AF900262

# SIDREA Series in Accounting and Business Administration


**Series Editors**

Stefano Marasca, Università Politecnica delle Marche, Ancona, Italy

Anna Maria Fellegara, Università Cattolica del Sacro Cuore, Piacenza, Italy

Riccardo Mussari, Università di Siena, Siena, Italy

**Editorial Board Members**

Stefano Adamo, Dipartimento di Studi Aziendali, G, Università degli studi di Lecce, LECCE, Italy

Luca Bartocci, University of Perugia, Perugia, Italy

Adele Caldarelli, University of Naples Federico II, Naples, Italy

Bettina Campedelli, University of Verona, Verona, Italy

Nicola Castellano, University of Pisa, Pisa, Italy

Denita Cepiku, University of Rome Tor Vergata, Rome, Italy

Lino Cinquini, Sant'Anna School of Advanced Studies, Pisa, Pisa, Italy

Maria Serena Chiucchi, DM, Marche Polytechnic University, Ancona, Italy

Vittorio Dell'Atti, University of Bari Aldo Moro, Bari, Italy

Francesco De Luca, University of Chieti-Pescara, PESCARA, Pescara, Italy

Anna Maria Fellegara, Catholic University of the Sacred Heart, PIACENZA, Piacenza, Italy

Raffaele Fiorentino, University of Naples Parthenope, Naples, Italy

Francesco Giunta, University of Florence, Florence, Italy

Alberto Incollingo, University of Campania "Luigi Vanvitelli, Caserta, Italy

Giovanni Liberatore, University of Florence, Florence, Italy

Andrea Lionzo, Economic & Business Management Science, Universita Cattolica del Sacro Cuore, MILANO, Milano, Italy

Rosa Lombardi, Law and Economics of Productive Activiti, Sapienza University of Rome, Roma, Italy

Davide Maggi, University of Eastern Piedmont Amadeo Av, Novara, Italy

Daniela Mancini, Campus "Aurelio Saliceti", University of Teramo, Teramo, Italy

Francesca Manes Rossi, University of Naples Federico II, Naples, Italy

Luciano Marchi, Dipto di Economia e Mgmt, University of Pisa, Pisa, Italy

Riccardo Mussari, University of Siena, Siena, Italy

Marco Maria Mattei, Department of Management, University of Bologna, Forlì, Italy

Antonella Paolini, University of Macerata, Macerata, Italy

Mauro Paoloni, University of Rome Tor Vergata, ROMA, Roma, Italy

Paola Paoloni, Dept Law & Econ of Productive Activities, Sapienza University of Rome, Rome, Roma, Italy

Marcantonio Ruisi, Dept SEAS, Buiding 13, University of Palermo, Palermo, Italy

Claudio Teodori, University of Brescia, Brescia, Italy

Simone Terzani, University of Perugia, Perugia, Italy

stefania veltri, DISCAG, Università della Calabria, RENDE, Cosenza, Italy

This is the official book series of SIDREA - the Italian Society of Accounting and Business Administration. This book series is provided with a wide Scientific Committee composed of Academics by SIDREA. It publishes contributions (monographs, edited volumes and proceedings) as a result of the double blind review process by the SIDREA's thematic research groups, operating at the national and international levels. Particularly, the series aims to disseminate specialized findings on several topics – classical and cutting-edge alike – that are currently being discussed by the accounting and business administration communities. The series authors are respected researchers and professors in the fields of business valuation; governance and internal control; financial accounting; public accounting; management control; gender; turnaround predictive models; non-financial disclosure; intellectual capital, smart technologies, and digitalization; and university governance and performance measurement.

Paolo Tenuta • Domenico Rocco Cambrea

# Corporate Sustainability

## Measurement, Reporting and Effects on Firm Performance

Springer

Paolo Tenuta
University of Calabria
Arcavacata di Rende, Italy

Domenico Rocco Cambrea
University of Modena and Reggio Emilia
Reggio Emilia, Italy

ISSN 2662-9879 ISSN 2662-9887 (electronic)
SIDREA Series in Accounting and Business Administration
ISBN 978-3-031-11490-8 ISBN 978-3-031-11491-5 (eBook)
https://doi.org/10.1007/978-3-031-11491-5

© The Editor(s) (if applicable) and The Author(s), under exclusive license to Springer Nature Switzerland AG 2022
This work is subject to copyright. All rights are solely and exclusively licensed by the Publisher, whether the whole or part of the material is concerned, specifically the rights of translation, reprinting, reuse of illustrations, recitation, broadcasting, reproduction on microfilms or in any other physical way, and transmission or information storage and retrieval, electronic adaptation, computer software, or by similar or dissimilar methodology now known or hereafter developed.
The use of general descriptive names, registered names, trademarks, service marks, etc. in this publication does not imply, even in the absence of a specific statement, that such names are exempt from the relevant protective laws and regulations and therefore free for general use.
The publisher, the authors, and the editors are safe to assume that the advice and information in this book are believed to be true and accurate at the date of publication. Neither the publisher nor the authors or the editors give a warranty, expressed or implied, with respect to the material contained herein or for any errors or omissions that may have been made. The publisher remains neutral with regard to jurisdictional claims in published maps and institutional affiliations.

This Springer imprint is published by the registered company Springer Nature Switzerland AG
The registered company address is: Gewerbestrasse 11, 6330 Cham, Switzerland

# Acknowledgements

We thank the Società Italiana dei Docenti di Ragioneria e di Economia Aziendale (SIDREA) and the anonymous reviewers for their valuable comments. We also would like to thank Professor Franco Ernesto Rubino for his helpful advice and Dr. Tonia Tassone for the support in researching the data used in the empirical analysis. Finally, a warm thank you to the Springer staff, particularly Rocio Torregrosa, for her great availability and professionalism. *This book is published in SIDREA Book Series "Accounting and Business Administration" edited by Springer as a result of the double-blind review process.*

# Contents

**1 Introduction** . . . . . 1
References . . . . . 4

**2 Principles and Practices of Sustainability** . . . . . 7
1 Business Ethics . . . . . 7
2 Corporate Social Responsibility . . . . . 10
3 Sustainability and Sustainable Development . . . . . 14
4 Corporate Sustainability . . . . . 15
5 Circular Economy and Sustainability . . . . . 17
References . . . . . 19

**3 ESG Measures and Non-financial Performance Reporting** . . . . . 27
1 Sustainability Indicators . . . . . 27
2 The ESG Rating . . . . . 29
3 The Main ESG Rating Agencies . . . . . 32
4 The Main ESG Indexes . . . . . 34
5 Non-financial Performance Reporting . . . . . 36
6 The Social and Environmental Balance . . . . . 37
7 The Sustainability Report . . . . . 42
8 The Integrated Report . . . . . 47
9 Directive 2014/95/EU and Proposal for the Directive CSRD 2021/0104 . . . . . 50
10 The Sustainability Disclosure Standards (ISSB Standards) . . . . . 51
References . . . . . 52

**4 Corporate Sustainability and Financial Performance** . . . . . 59
1 Introduction . . . . . 59
2 Literature Review and Research Hypotheses . . . . . 61
2.1 Sustainability Performance and Financial Performance . . . . . 61
2.2 Sustainability Performance and Financial Performance in Family and Nonfamily Firms . . . . . 63

2.3 Collegial Leadership . . . . . 64
3 Methodology . . . . . 66
3.1 Data Collection and Sample . . . . . 66
3.2 Dependent Variable . . . . . 66
3.3 Independent and Moderating Variables . . . . . 66
3.4 Control Variables . . . . . 67
3.5 Model . . . . . 67
4 Analysis and Results . . . . . 68
4.1 Descriptive Analysis . . . . . 68
4.2 Hypotheses Testing . . . . . 68
5 Discussion . . . . . 72
References . . . . . 74

**5 Future Research Directions** . . . . . 81

**6 Conclusions** . . . . . 83
References . . . . . 85

# Chapter 1
# Introduction

**Abstract** This part illustrates the main themes discussed in the book. Specifically, the topics developed in the three chapters are reviewed, highlighting the most significant aspects for business administration scholars and the main results that will be analyzed in detail in the sections of the book.

In recent years, corporate social responsibility (CSR) and Corporate Sustainability (CS) practices have been at the center of a debate. The increased interest in CSR and CS issues has notably increased studies in these areas (Chatterji et al., 2009).

The terms CSR, Environmental, Social and Government (ESG) and CS are often used alternatively (Khattak, 2021). The expressions "sustainable development" or "sustainability" (Waas et al., 2011) and CSR and ESG, although based on different theories, are considered standard terms in the literature (do Prado et al., 2020). Previous studies have discussed the convergence or autonomy of the two terms CSR and CS (Ashrafi et al., 2018). Montiel (2008) reviews the different definitions of CSR and CS and clarifies that the managerial literature uses the two terms to refer to "issues to social and environmental management issues, but there is no clear distinction." Although there are points of difference between the two constructs, conceptualizations and measures of CSR and CS seem to converge. Both the aspects share the same vision to balance the economic sphere with the social and environmental one. However, CS scholars argue that economic, social, and environmental factors are interrelated, while a relevant part of the empirical research on CSR treats economic and social performance as independent components. In CSR, environmental issues are a subset of social performance, whereas in CS, they represent an independent element. The conceptualization of CSR and that of the triple bottom line of CS are very similar. "Both show that companies need to balance the three elements to achieve sustainability and social responsibility results. Both CSR and CS aim to balance economic prosperity, social integrity, and environmental responsibility, regardless of whether they conceptualize environmental issues as a subset of social issues or as the third element of sustainability."

This paper will consider the triple bottom line and CSR as similar approaches to the same philosophy of sustainability (do Prado et al., 2020).

© The Author(s), under exclusive license to Springer Nature Switzerland AG 2022 
P. Tenuta, D. R. Cambrea, *Corporate Sustainability*, SIDREA Series in Accounting and Business Administration, https://doi.org/10.1007/978-3-031-11491-5_1

In recent decades, the notion of CSR has given rise to a competing institutional logic that has led companies to comply with rules other than those required by law or by the market (Mintzberg, 1983), modifying the role of investors. Investors who traditionally were seen as interested only in profit act as the engine of institutional change towards CSR (Hutton et al., 1998).

The spread of sustainable and responsible investment (SRI), which requires reliable data on the ESG performance of various companies, changes the institutional context for companies, allowing investors to favor socially responsible ones to the detriment of those that are not (Avetisyan & Hockerts, 2017; Hockerts & Moir, 2004). The request for accurate information, not only from a financial point of view but also from an ESG point of view, has become part of companies' competitive strategy (Galbreath, 2013). Furthermore, the Sustainable Development Goals (SDGs) have a macro-approach that makes their application difficult at the company level. All this has led to the proliferation of indexes and ratings that measure sustainability, often expressed in terms of environmental, social and governance (ESG) (Diez-Cañamero et al., 2020).

For these reasons, it is becoming increasingly essential for companies to measure and report on their non-financial performance.

Based on these premises, we analyze the theories related to the concepts of CSR, CS, sustainable development, and circular economy (CE). Subsequently, we verify the practices related to the rating and the formation of ESG indexes and the tools for reporting non-financial performance and, finally, using the ESG rating of a recognized agency, we verify the link between CS and corporate financial performance also concerning the distinction between family and nonfamily firms.

The book is divided into three chapters in which the theoretical aspects are treated first and then the practical implications relating to CS practices.

In the first chapter, we mainly analyze the issues of CSR and CS as they are driving factors of sustainability and general well-being (Moon, 2007; Montiel, 2008), focusing on the concept of circular economy (CE) as a critical element in the transition towards a more sustainable future. The idea of CSR appears to be interconnected with that of sustainable development, as social responsibility is nothing more than the contribution that companies make to sustainable development. Leading businesses towards sustainability require a change in conceiving and measuring one's performance. "The transition to a circular economy is a step towards sustainability" (Aboulamer, 2018). To do this, it is necessary to think in terms of triple bottom lines, that is, to adopt management methods aimed at jointly maximizing the three economic, social, and environmental dimensions (Eccles & Krzus, 2010). Millar et al. (2019) believe that the CE approach is central to the debate on sustainability policy. The CE, in fact, helps to attain the three dimensions (economic, social, and environmental) of sustainable development (Korhonen et al., 2018; Schroeder et al., 2019). CE innovations are seen as a component in companies' broader attempt to move towards CSR and sustainability (Reif & Rexhäuser, 2018). For these reasons, the CE has gained increasing attention (Lieder & Rashid, 2016) and academic articles and practical proposals around the concept of CE have increased significantly (Geisendorf & Pietrulla, 2018).

In the second chapter, we analyze the ways of measuring CS and the evolution of social and environmental disclosure (SED) that have taken place from the 1970s to today. Sustainability is a multidimensional concept for which evaluating the performance of companies in terms of sustainability must take into account various ESG criteria (Liern & Pérez-Gladish, 2018). It becomes increasingly essential, therefore, to measure financial and non-financial performance. According to Avetisyan and Ferrary (2013), the change is evident from the emergence of ESG rating agencies that provide the same services like credit rating agencies but refer to ESG criteria. This is the result of sustainable and responsible investment (SRI), which are consolidated due to the possible positive correlation found in various studies between CS practices and corporate financial performance (Brooks & Oikonomou, 2018). Following the approach used by Avetisyan and Ferrary (2013) we use as a source of data the information provided on the official websites of ESG rating agencies, from previous scientific articles and the websites of the major companies present in the ratings and indexes analyzed. The aim is to identify the prominent rating companies and the most widespread ESG indexes and facilitate companies and investors in selecting organizations. We provide them with information on the origins, historical evolution, and structure of the main rating agencies and the most popular ESG indexes (Avetisyan & Ferrary, 2013). Previous authors have already analyzed ESG rating agencies (Escrig-Olmedo et al., 2019), their strategies (Avetisyan & Hockerts, 2017), their evaluation processes and weighing systems (Chatterji et al., 2016; Escrig-Olmedo et al., 2010). However, few studies explore the origins, historical evolution, or structure of ESG rating agencies (Avetisyan & Hockerts, 2017) and whether these ratings are accurate (Chatterji et al., 2016). We fill this gap by analyzing the leading rating agencies and the main existing ESG indexes. We also examine the evolution of social and environmental disclosure (SED), which can be considered an example of corporate social and environmental sustainability (Martin-Sardesai & Guthrie, 2020). Attention to non-financial information is rising, as numerous studies claim (Ioannou & Serafeim, 2015; Luo et al., 2015). Let's examine the reporting documents starting from the classic models that separate financial information from non-financial information and then move on to integrated models (Venturelli et al., 2017), which include both types of information to provide stakeholders with overall summary data on the company's performance (Maas et al., 2016). The second chapter ends with the description of the proposal for the Corporate Sustainability Reporting Directive (CSRD) 2021/0104, with which the European Commission sets itself the ultimate goal of bringing sustainability reporting to the same level as financial reporting by strengthening the existing rules.

In the third chapter, through an empirical analysis, we verify the impact of CS, measured through ESG performance, on corporate financial performance also with reference to the distinction between family and nonfamily firms. According to Aboulamer (2018), previous studies on the relationship between CS and its financial performance provide conflicting results that leave room for further investigation. The different results are often related to measuring sustainability performance (Horváthová, 2010; Endrikat et al., 2014; Lu et al., 2014; Wang et al., 2016). Furthermore, much of the research focuses on the US market and only a few studies have been conducted on European markets (Nuber et al., 2020; Friede et al., 2015), in Germany (Nuber et al., 2020) or in Italy (Provasi & Harasheh, 2021). The issue of family businesses, on the other hand, has been much debated in relation to financial performance but not in terms of sustainability performance. Despite the numerous studies in the literature, few empirical researchers examine family businesses (Broccardo et al., 2019), especially in some contexts where they are the vast majority of companies listed on the stock exchange (García-Ramos & García-Olalla, 2011; Acquaah, 2013; Chrisman et al., 2014; Singal & Gerde, 2015). In this regard, there are numerous reports in the literature about the need to feed studies on the link between family businesses and sustainability performance (Adomako et al., 2019; Broccardo et al., 2019).

Therefore, based on these considerations, this research aims to verify the evolution of CS practices, their reporting, and how this impact can be measured through the proliferation of rating agencies and numerous ESG indexes in recent years. Furthermore, given the uncertainty and discrepancy of the inconclusive results in the literature, we verify the existence of a significant relationship between the level of CS and corporate financial performance also concerning the distinction between family and non-family firms.

## References


Aboulamer, A. (2018). Adopting a circular business model improves market equity value. *Thunderbird International Business Review, 60*(5), 765–769. https://doi.org/10.1002/tie.21922

Acquaah, M. (2013). Management control systems, business strategy and performance: A comparative analysis of family and non-family businesses in a transition economy in sub-Saharan Africa. *Journal of Family Business Strategy, 4*(2), 131–146. https://doi.org/10.1016/j.jfbs.2013.03.002

Adomako, S., Amankwah-Amoah, J., Danso, A., Konadu, R., & Owusu-Agyei, S. (2019). Environmental sustainability orientation and performance of family and nonfamily firms. *Business Strategy and the Environment, 28*(6), 1250–1259. https://doi.org/10.1002/bse.2314

Ashrafi, M., Adams, M., Walker, T. R., & Magnan, G. (2018). How corporate social responsibility can be integrated into corporate sustainability: A theoretical review of their relationships. *International Journal of Sustainable Development & World Ecology, 25*(8), 672–682. https://doi.org/10.1080/13504509.2018.1471628

Avetisyan, E., & Ferrary, M. (2013). Dynamics of stakeholders' implications in the institutionalization of the CSR field in France and in the United States. *Journal of Business Ethics, 115*(1), 115–133. https://doi.org/10.1007/s10551-012-1386-3

Avetisyan, E., & Hockerts, K. (2017). The consolidation of the ESG rating industry as an enactment of institutional retrogression. *Business Strategy and the Environment, 26*(3), 316–330. https://doi.org/10.1002/bse.1919

Broccardo, L., Truant, E., & Zicari, A. (2019). Internal corporate sustainability drivers: What evidence from family firms? A literature review and research agenda. *Corporate Social Responsibility and Environmental Management, 26*(1), 1–18. https://doi.org/10.1002/csr.1672

Brooks, C., & Oikonomou, I. (2018). The effects of environmental, social and governance disclosures and performance on firm value: A review of the literature in accounting and finance. *British Accounting Review, 50*(1), 1–15. https://doi.org/10.1016/j.bar.2017.11.005

Chatterji, A. K., Durand, R., Levine, D. I., & Touboul, S. (2016). Do ratings of firms converge? Implications for managers, investors and strategy researchers. *Strategic Management Journal, 37*, 1597–1614. https://doi.org/10.1002/smj.2407

Chatterji, A. K., Levine, D. I., & Toffel, M. W. (2009). How well do social ratings actually measure corporate social responsibility? *Journal of Economics and Management Strategy, 18*(1), 125–169. https://doi.org/10.1111/j.1530-9134.2009.00210.x

Chrisman, J. J., Memili, E., & Misra, K. (2014). Nonfamily managers, family firms, and the winner's curse: The influence of noneconomic goals and bounded rationality. *Entrepreneurship: Theory and Practice, 38*(5), 1103–1127. https://doi.org/10.1111/etap.12014

Diez-Cañamero, B., Bishara, T., Otegi-Olaso, J. R., Minguez, R., & Fernández, J. M. (2020). Measurement of corporate social responsibility: A review of corporate sustainability indexes, rankings and ratings. *Sustainability, 12*(5). https://doi.org/10.3390/su12052153

do Prado, G. F., Piekarski, C. M., da Luz, L. M., de Souza, J. T., Salvador, R., & de Francisco, A. C. (2020). Sustainable development and economic performance: Gaps and trends for future research. *Sustainable Development, 28*(1), 368–384. https://doi.org/10.1002/sd.1982

Eccles, R. G., & Krzus, M. P. (2010). *One report: Integrated reporting for a sustainable strategy*. John Wiley & Sons.

Endrikat, J., Guenther, E., & Hoppe, H. (2014). Making sense of conflicting empirical findings: A meta-analytic review of the relationship between corporate environmental and financial performance. *European Management Journal, 32*(5), 735–751. https://doi.org/10.1016/j.emj.2013.12.004

Escrig-Olmedo, E., Fernández-Izquierdo, M., Ferrero-Ferrero, I., Rivera-Lirio, J. M., & Muñoz-Torres, M. J. (2019). Rating the raters: Evaluating how ESG rating agencies integrate sustainability principles. *Sustainability, 11*(3). https://doi.org/10.3390/su11030915

Escrig-Olmedo, E., Muñoz-Torres, M. J., & Fernandez-Izquierdo, M. A. (2010). Socially responsible investing: Sustainability indices, ESG rating and information provider agencies. *International Journal Sustainable Econonomy, 2*, 442–461.

Friede, G., Busch, T., & Bassen, A. (2015). ESG and financial performance: Aggregated evidence from more than 2000 empirical studies. *Journal of Sustainable Finance and Investment, 5*(4), 210–233. https://doi.org/10.1080/20430795.2015.1118917

Galbreath, J. (2013). ESG in focus: The Australian evidence. *Journal of Business Ethics, 118*(3), 529–541. https://doi.org/10.1007/s10551-012-1607-9

García-Ramos, R., & García-Olalla, M. (2011). Board characteristics and firm performance in public founder–and nonfounder-led family businesses. *Journal of Family Business Strategy, 2*(4), 220–231. https://doi.org/10.1016/j.jfbs.2011.09.001

Geisendorf, S., & Pietrulla, F. (2018). The circular economy and circular economic concepts–a literature analysis and redefinition. *Thunderbird International Business Review, 60*(5), 771–782. https://doi.org/10.1002/tie.21924

Hockerts, K., & Moir, L. (2004). Communicating corporate responsibility to investors: The changing role of the investor relations function. *Journal of Business Ethics, 52*(1), 85–98. https://doi.org/10.1023/B:BUSI.0000033109.35980.16

Horváthová, E. (2010). Does environmental performance affect financial performance? *A meta-analysis. Ecological Economics, 70*(1), 52–59. https://doi.org/10.1016/j.ecolecon.2010.04.004

Hutton, R. B., D'Antonio, L., & Johnsen, T. (1998). Socially responsible investing: Growing issues and new opportunities. *Business & Society., 37*(3), 281–305. https://doi.org/10.1177/000765039803700303

Ioannou, I., & Serafeim, G. (2015). The impact of corporate social responsibility on investment recommendations: Analysts' perceptions and shifting institutional logics. *Strategic Management Journal, 36*(7), 1053–1081. https://doi.org/10.1002/smj.2268

Khattak, M. A. (2021). Corporate sustainability and financial performance of banks in Muslim economies: The role of institutions. *Journal of Public Affairs, 21*(1). https://doi.org/10.1002/pa.2156

Korhonen, J., Nuur, C., Feldmann, A., & Birkie, S. E. (2018). Circular economy as an essentially contested concept. *Journal of Cleaner Production, 175*, 544–552. https://doi.org/10.1016/j.jclepro.2017.12.111

Lieder, M., & Rashid, A. (2016). Towards circular economy implementation: A comprehensive review in context of manufacturing industry. *Journal of Cleaner Production, 115*, 36–51. Elsevier Ltd. https://doi.org/10.1016/j.jclepro.2015.12.042

Liern, V., & Pérez-Gladish, B. (2018). Ranking corporate sustainability: A flexible multidimensional approach based on linguistic variables. *International Transactions in Operational Research, 25*(3), 1081–1100. https://doi.org/10.1111/itor.12469

Lu, W., Chau, K. W., Wang, H., & Pan, W. (2014). A decade's debate on the nexus between corporate social and corporate financial performance: A critical review of empirical studies 2002-2011. *Journal of Cleaner Production, 79*, 195–206. https://doi.org/10.1016/j.jclepro.2014.04.072

Luo, X., Wang, H., Raithel, S., & Zheng, Q. (2015). Corporate social performance, analyst stock recommendations, and firm future returns. *Strategic Management Journal, 36*(1), 123–136. https://doi.org/10.1002/smj.2219

Maas, K., Schaltegger, S., & Crutzen, N. (2016). Integrating corporate sustainability assessment, management accounting, control, and reporting. *Journal of Cleaner Production, 136*, 237–248. https://doi.org/10.1016/j.jclepro.2016.05.008

Martin-Sardesai, A., & Guthrie, J. (2020). Social report innovation: Evidence from a major Italian bank 2007-2012. *Meditari Accountancy Research, 28*(1), 72–88. https://doi.org/10.1108/MEDAR-10-2018-0383

Millar, N., McLaughlin, E., & Börger, T. (2019). The circular economy: Swings and roundabouts? *Ecological Economics, 158*, 11–19. https://doi.org/10.1016/j.ecolecon.2018.12.012

Mintzberg, H. (1983). The case for corporate social responsibility. *Journal of Business Strategy, 4*(2), 3–15. https://doi.org/10.1108/eb039015

Montiel, I. (2008). Corporate social responsibility and corporate sustainability: Separate pasts, common futures. *Organization and Environment, 21*(3), 245–269. https://doi.org/10.1177/1086026608321329

Moon, J. (2007). The contribution of corporate social responsibility to sustainable development. *Sustainable Development, 15*(5), 296–306. https://doi.org/10.1002/sd.346

Nuber, C., Velte, P., & Hörisch, J. (2020). The curvilinear and time-lagging impact of sustainability performance on financial performance: Evidence from Germany. *Corporate Social Responsibility and Environmental Management, 27*(1), 232–243. https://doi.org/10.1002/csr.1795

Provasi, R., & Harasheh, M. (2021). Gender diversity and corporate performance: Emphasis on sustainability performance. *Corporate Social Responsibility and Environmental Management, 28*(1), 127–137. https://doi.org/10.1002/csr.2037

Reif, C., & Rexhäuser, S. (2018). In J. Horbach & C. Reif (Eds.), *Good enough! Are socially responsible companies the more successful environmental innovators?* Springer. https://doi.org/10.1007/978-3-319-93019-0_8

Schroeder, P., Anggraeni, K., & Weber, U. (2019). The relevance of circular economy practices to the sustainable development goals. *Journal of Industrial Ecology, 23*(1), 77–95. https://doi.org/10.1111/jiec.12732

Singal, M., & Gerde, V. W. (2015). Is diversity management related to financial performance in family firms? *Family Business Review, 28*(3), 243–259. https://doi.org/10.1177/0894486514566012

Venturelli, A., Caputo, F., Cosma, S., Leopizzi, R., & Pizzi, S. (2017). Directive 2014/95/EU: Are Italian companies already compliant? *Sustainability, 9*(8). https://doi.org/10.3390/su9081385

Waas, T., Hugé, J., Verbruggen, A., & Wright, T. (2011). Sustainable development: A bird's eye view. *Sustainability, 3*(10), 1637–1661. https://doi.org/10.3390/su3101637

Wang, Q., Dou, J., & Jia, S. (2016). A meta-analytic review of corporate social responsibility and corporate financial performance: The moderating effect of contextual factors. *Business and Society, 55*(8), 1083–1121. https://doi.org/10.1177/0007650315584317

# Chapter 2
# Principles and Practices of Sustainability

**Abstract** In the first chapter, we introduce the general topics related to sustainability concepts. In doing so, we review the main studies on Corporate Social Responsibility (CSR) and Corporate Sustainability (CS) subjects. The section provides a detailed explanation of the several arguments related to the corporate sustainability, describing the relationships between business ethics, corporate social responsibility, and sustainable development.

Based on the idea that corporate social responsibility is interconnected with sustainable development and general well-being, this chapter clarifies the concept of circular economy as a critical element in the transition towards a more sustainable future. The work identifies the central role of the circular economy in the debate on sustainability policy since it helps attain the three dimensions (economic, social, and environmental) of sustainable development. We review the sustainability principles and classify the management methods necessary to operate following a triple bottom approach according to what the companies should adopt for jointly maximizing the three contextual dimensions (economic, social, and environmental). In this way, the work presents the circular economy innovations as an essential tool for helping companies move toward CSR and sustainability.

## 1 Business Ethics

The phenomena of internationalization and globalization of the markets have led to a situation that has seen companies compete in more expansive areas than the usual national realities. Companies necessarily had to confront and analyze new markets, products, human resources, strategies, and financial instruments (Hinna, 2005). Businesses find themselves facing a context in which balance and business success no longer derive exclusively from the pursuit of income but from compliance with an integrated approach that must necessarily consider the ethical aspect of their management (Allen, 2001; Cassidy, 2003; Catturi, 2003; Borgonovi & Rusconi, 2008).

According to Adam Smith (1759), self-interest should be moderated by ethics. In this way, purely selfish behavior would be the exception and not the rule. This would ensure respect for individual rights and justice while making a profit (Bowie, 1995).

© The Author(s), under exclusive license to Springer Nature Switzerland AG 2022

P. Tenuta, D. R. Cambrea, *Corporate Sustainability*, SIDREA Series in Accounting and Business Administration, https://doi.org/10.1007/978-3-031-11491-5_2

These are the foundations that have led companies in all sectors to affirm the principles of respect for ethics, society, and the environment by investing in the quality of the relationship with workers, in the trust of consumers and savers, and the reputation of the market (Camilleri, 2017). These issues developed in the United States and then spread to all advanced countries assuming that ethics does not consist only in respecting the laws but in giving oneself some rules that form the basis of business management (Birindelli & Taraballa, 2001). Business ethics is conceived as the study of the set of principles, values, and ethical norms that govern economic activities (Sacconi & Baldin, 2003). According to Chirieleison (2002), companies were interested in socially responsible behavior often out of fear of social control in the past. Subsequently, the line of studies on business ethics was based on two assumptions: an analysis of the values on which corporate decisions must be based and the definition of rules of conduct that inform about management and the related control system.

The term ethics refers to customs, habits, and individual behavior. The purpose of ethics and morals is to illuminate and guide the life of men in terms of good and justice (Rusconi & Dorigatti, 2004). This has translated into companies' real cultural turning point, an evolution in their management mentality, and a real leap in quality (Dalle & Bounine, 1975).

The complexity of the relationships between the economic unit and the social environment is based on the development of business ethics, or rather on a system of values, which acts as a reference for the orientation of the business choices (Gagliardi, 1995). These are external rules of conduct inherent to business-environment relations, and internal behavior rules regarding company management and non-executive personnel (Cavalieri, 2002). On the internal side, business ethics allows for the creation of strong relationships between the company and its employees, such as to which the values of person and worker are recognized, thus building a path of growth for the company, parallel to the growth path of the person who works there. On the external side, business ethics contributes to creating a moral cohesion that leads to pursuing the general interest with profit (Rija & Tenuta, 2010).

The pursuit of the corporate purpose and the creation of value, translated in terms of long-term objectives and cost-effectiveness, cannot disregard principles, values, and ethical norms that guarantee the integration of the company into the cultural and social environment in which it lives and operates. This allows us to understand whether or not there is a consonance between the philosophy of the company and the company and to evaluate the level of social consensus that the company can obtain (Mazzoleni, 2006). Profit simply ceases to be considered as a priority to be invested with fundamental social relevance. In fact, it allows companies to last over time, be autonomous to develop and generate value for the future and ensure an economic and financial balance. However, this does not imply that companies can do without the profit that is basic to make those investments, without which the company would lose its competitive ability. The company is a subject endowed with its purpose: to carry out its economic activity, favoring the respect for the customer/user and attention to his needs and enhancement of all resources used (human, financial, infrastructural, environmental). Profit assumes importance as a fundamental consequence of the achievement of the corporate mission. It will therefore be up to the management to trigger and keep the virtuous circuits functioning that drive business development (Rapport, 1989). The economically excellent company must be socially capable of assuming the joint pursuit of economic value and social value as its objective. This fundamental mix ensures the achievement of results consistent with its desire to last over time and at the same time satisfy the expectations of all stakeholders (Bufera & Catino, 2002). The basic idea is that to create value; it is necessary to achieve a positive financial performance that derives from a satisfactory economic result that can be achieved through achieving a differential competitive advantage with respect to competitors (Carnevale, 2005).

Therefore, the company must be able to interface ethically with the problems that arise as a prerequisite for a broader CSR. This has resulted in the adoption of ethical codes containing moral rules and values on which the corporate culture is based, as well as the policies regarding corporate ethics, the rules of conduct to be adapted and the rules of responsibility towards stakeholders. This tool, emerging in the United States in the last century, is the basis on which to establish stable and advantageous relationships of trust between the company and its interlocutors, as well as the reference for expressing judgments on the reliability and good reputation of the same (Beda & Bodo, 2006). The code of ethics is the main tool for implementing ethics within the company (Kaptein & Schwartz, 2008; Singh, 2011; Webley & Werner, 2008) because it introduces an unequivocal definition of corporate ethical and social responsibilities. Companies have decided to make use of a code of ethics to establish a climate of trust on the part of the customer regarding the quality of the services and goods offered (De Waegeneer et al., 2016). Companies have adopted ethical codes in the belief that corporate behavior, correct from the ethical point of view, could turn into a competitive advantage (Porter & Kramer, 2006).

Although numerous analyses have investigated the effectiveness of such ethical codes, the results remain inconclusive (Helin & Sandström, 2007; Kaptein & Schwartz, 2008). Applying the code of ethics has been positively seen in most cases as it can eliminate the incorrect practices that cause customer losses and short- and long-term economic losses. Furthermore, adopting ethical codes clarifies the margins of ethical uncertainty found in company policies and offers alternative methods of conduct to introduce new rules in the existing motivation and incentive mechanisms (Coda, 1996). A code of ethics also represents a useful communication tool within the company, towards employees and externally with all subjects linked to economic activity. This document contains a series of rules that act as a communication tool between the company and its stakeholders on environmental, social and governance policies (Saygili & Öztürkoğlu, 2017) and direct the company's action on morally correct values (Viviani, 2006).

Ethics and CSR have become increasingly analyzed elements in recent decades. Ethics is often defined as "doing good" and interrelated with CSR (Schwartz & Carroll, 2008). Most research considers corporate ethics and CSR integrated and overlapping (Brunk, 2012). The academic community has often combined business ethics and CSR (Ferrell et al., 2019).

Following corporate scandals, many studies have focused on issues such as corporate fraud, abuse of executive power, and corporate social irresponsibility. As a result, companies were forced to take into account the externalities arising from their business. Therefore, CSR and ethics have become essential elements to remain competitive, unlike the traditional corporate approach that aims to profit without considering social and environmental impacts (Lo & Sheu, 2007).

The ethical and profit aspects must coexist in every company and be balanced (Orlitzky et al., 2011). Numerous studies have reversed traditional views that ethical practices are costly and negatively correlated with returns (Reinhardt, 2017). Pae and Choi (2011) find that ethical companies can increase their business value by reducing the cost of equity. Furthermore, Joner and Payne (2002) observe that business ethics positively impact the performance of companies and are indispensable in modern business contexts.

Consequently, we must also look at the ethical aspect to understand positive company performance. A more ethical and transparent way of business management is widely discussed in the literature (Tenuta, 2009). If CSR is a candidate as the main means capable of ensuring the survival and continued success of its business for any organization, the fact that it, as well as any other self-respecting distinctive resource or competence, needs to be managed and communicated efficiently without any misleading. The purpose of ethics and morals is to illuminate the life of men in terms of good and justice (Rusconi & Dorigatti, 2004). A company's management can be defined as ethical only in the presence of integration between the economic, social, and environmental aspects (Gray et al., 1996).

## 2 Corporate Social Responsibility

Despite the widespread interest in CSR issues and its long and diverse history (Borgonovi et al., 2017; Mussari & Monfardini, 2010; Carroll, 1999), a standard definition is still lacking in the literature (van Marrewijk & Werre, 2003). According to Lo and Sheu (2007), a classic view of the stakeholder approach is that a company's social responsibility is to increase its profits.

As the first approximation, it may seem that, if the market works well and fairly reflects the expectations of those who work there, the real social duty of the company is to try to obtain as much stable profit as possible in the long term, respecting the laws and current morals. Therefore, one might think that, for social purposes, the financial statements and the code of ethics are enough. Instead, it should be noted that we cannot speak of modern business management if we neglect the relational aspects that involve companies. Indeed, long-term competitive success cannot be lasting if the social interlocutors and their legitimate expectations are not taken into consideration, which increasingly affects the social and environmental sphere and the economic one. Furthermore, some aspects necessary for the stakeholders for knowledge purposes, such as choices of principles or moral values, do not emerge from the financial statements, just as some costs/benefits for the community deriving from the activity carried out do not emerge.

For several years, companies have understood that in order to operate successfully, it is necessary not only to achieve excellent competitive-income performance, but also to fulfill social purposes. What the company is asked to offer is not only a product with an excellent quality-price ratio but, above all, a product capable of causing a low environmental impact and such as to guarantee, to the people who proceed to its realization, "fair pay associated with healthy working conditions" (Molteni, 2004).

CSR theory holds that an organization faces distinct aspects rather than just providing profit to its shareholders. An organization must address the economic and legal aspects by respecting local legislation, the ethical aspect by acting ethically towards the market and the philanthropic aspect by providing society with elements that it could not otherwise benefit from (Carroll, 1999).

The term CSR refers to an enlarged corporate governance model. The person who governs the company has responsibilities from the observance of fiduciary duties towards the property to analogous fiduciary duties towards the stakeholders (Bertoli, 2007; Terzani, 1984; Matacena, 1984; Bandettini, 1981; Cavalieri, 1981). Being socially responsible does not only mean respecting legal obligations (Mintzberg, 1983), but also investing more in human capital, in the environment and in relations with other interested parties (Cavicchi, 2003). Through CSR policies, the "social" aspect of one's company is not only improved, but a quantifiable return is obtained in competitive advantage (Burke & Logsdon, 1996; Lantos, 2001; Sen et al., 2006) aimed at positively influencing the performance of the company with a view to development. The reputation that comes from ethical management of the company allows stakeholders to trust, be satisfied in their work, and cooperate with it (Sacconi & Baldin, 2003), which will influence the market price of its shares (Chami et al., 2002). While carrying out their business, companies must consider the needs of the stakeholders and operate in order to create consensus and legitimacy. Business ethics, corporate citizenship, sustainability, and sustainable development are all concepts that are based on the logic according to which economic, social, and environmental aspects must be considered to evaluate the overall performance of a company (Ricci, 2010; Campedelli, 2005; Pulejo, 1996).

Although the idea that companies have a responsibility towards society is not new, it was only in the 1950s that the literature began to discuss the social responsibilities of companies.

The greater social attention to this issue has led to a change in the behavior of companies and in the very idea of CSR (Latapí Agudelo et al., 2019).

The concept of CSR was born in the 1950s in the United States (CSR1). It was based on the belief that the company should contribute to the economic, technological, and social progress of the territory in which it operates through the appropriate use of the bargaining power it holds. This definition, however, involved a compulsory assumption of social duties and ethical norms, and moreover, it impacted the management and administrative policies of the company, therefore encountering much criticism and ending up with a negative value. In this period, the first criticisms of CSR also arose. Friedman (1962) criticizes CSR by stating that accepting the CSR criterion instead of seeking the maximum return for shareholders undermines the foundations of a free society. This would represent an abuse, by managers, of the delegation received from the owners of the firm and aimed at making profits (Friedman, 1970). Levitt in 1958 and Friedman in 1962 argued that companies' only responsibility was to maximize shareholder wealth and not deal with social issues (Camilleri, 2017).

In the 1970s, Frederick (1994) developed a new concept of CSR, called Corporate Social Responsiveness (CSR2), with a more managerial basis than in the past (Chirieleison, 2002). With this concept, the level of sensitivity of companies is highlighted while the first tools were developed to measure and activate this sensitivity and responsibility. These include social auditing techniques, social balance sheets, ethical codes, and self-regulatory codes. But even this trend ended up being criticized as being too focused on these operational tools that neglect the most important aspect to be implemented, attributable to the implementation of ethical values that should have permeated the entire company system. In the 1980s, with the third line of studies called business ethics, we witnessed an evolution of the concept of CSR (CSR3) (Carnevale & Carnevale, 2008). According to Frederick (1986), business ethics affirm the *Corporate Social Rectitude*, which incorporates the implicit moral dimension in CSR1 and the managerial one in CSR2. But it is in the 1990s, we witnessed an evolution of the concept of CSR (Chirieleison, 2002), which led to an evaluation of the more general socially responsible conduct of the company, considered towards all stakeholders. This is how we arrived at an evolution of the stakeholder theory, which constitutes the starting point for reflection on the mechanisms through which the company obtains and loses its social legitimacy (Donaldson & Preston, 1995). The stakeholder theory, cited for the first time by Freeman, is based on the idea that closer ties and relationships of mutual influence are created between the company and the reference environment (Freeman, 1984). Freeman defines the stakeholder theory as a new single concept from the corporate responsibility, largely opposite to Friedman's classic vision according to which "there is one and only one social responsibility of business to use its resources and engage in activities designed to increase its profits so long as it stays within the rules of the game, which is to say, engages in open and free competition, without deception of fraud"(Friedman, 1962).

Diez-Cañamero et al. (2020) analyze the evolution of the concept of CSR and the convergence with stakeholder theory. From Bowen (2013), who links CSR with the social conscience of managers, to Frederick (1960), who takes a step forward and links CSR to the satisfaction of society in general, to McGuire (1963), who goes further by defining CSR as responsibility beyond legal obligations, to Walton (1982) who addresses CSR as a business–society relationship. At this point, according to the authors, CSR "already adopts a multi-stakeholder perspective converging with the stakeholder theory."

Already in the first definitions of stakeholders, we perceive the presence of a bond of dependence between them and the company. To develop in terms of competitiveness and profitability, we must consider the interests of all the interlocutors who are in a relationship with it. Considering these interests means moving from management policies aimed exclusively at the pursuit of profit to choices that aim to maximize the well-being of all stakeholders. Freeman distinguishes primary and secondary stakeholders based on the importance of their contribution to the survival of the organization (Freeman, 1984).

The stakeholder theory can be considered one of the main theoretical insights that have significantly contributed to the evolution of CSR (Chirieleison, 2002), a fundamental pillar of CSR (Diez-Cañamero et al., 2020). Carroll (1999) argues that the main contribution of the stakeholder theory is to conceive CSR as a process that leads the company to integrate socially responsible behavior into its activities. This makes CSR more concrete, which is linked to the various interests held by the stakeholders.

Therefore, the socially responsible company must adopt ethical and correct behavior both inside and outside the company, contributing to the improvement of the company and minimizing the environmental impact by going beyond compliance with regulatory provisions (Beda & Bodo, 2006; Bartocci, 2003; Gabrovec Mei, 2002; Rusconi, 1988; Pulejo, 1996). Therefore, as specified in the European Commission's Green Paper, there is an internal and an external dimension of social responsibility. The first includes the management of human resources, health and safety at work, adaptation to changes, and managing the effects on the environment and natural resources. The management of human resources must follow a series of adequate measures that take into account education and training throughout the lifespan, the empowerment of personnel, an improvement of the information circuit in the company, a better balance between work, family and leisure time, greater diversity of human resources, the application of the principle of equality for wages and career prospects for women, benefit-sharing and share ownership schemes, as well as taking into account the ability to "professional integration and safety in the workplace." Many companies have made an essential criterion of health and safety in the selection of the purchase of products and services from other companies and a marketing element for the sale of their products and services. These voluntary measures can be considered as an integration of the legislative and control activities of public authorities since these tools also tend to develop a culture of prevention, in other words, a better level of safety and health protection in the workplace.

Furthermore, restructuring from a socially responsible point of view means taking into account the interests of all parties involved in changes and decisions. Any such operation should be prepared, the risks must be identified, calculating all costs and evaluating all alternative solutions that can reduce redundancies. Finally, reducing the consumption of resources or the emissions of waste or pollutants can lead to a decrease in reflections on the environment. This strategy can benefit the company by reducing its energy bill and waste disposal costs and by reducing the cost of raw materials and generic measures against pollution.

The external dimension of CSR includes all those beyond the company's perimeter, that is, local communities, commercial partnerships, suppliers and consumers, human rights, and environmental concerns at a global level. Businesses contribute to the local community by providing jobs, wages, benefits, and tax revenues.

Conversely, businesses depend on their host communities' good health, stability, and prosperity. Another important factor affecting external social responsibility is business partnerships. Working in collaboration with commercial partners means reducing the complexity of operations and, above all costs, increasing quality. Commercial partnerships, therefore, in compliance with the provisions of EU and national competition law, certainly are elements capable of generating greater profits. About human rights, companies are increasingly adopting ethical codes of conduct relating to working conditions, human rights, environmental protection, and anti-corruption. Finally, global environmental concerns presuppose a general improvement in environmental performance. Companies can no longer stop exclusively at pursuing their market objectives. Together with the pursuit of income, companies must be driven by responsibility and consistency, integrity, fairness, transparency, the centrality of the person, in the belief that everything that is ethical and social responsibility represents the company's contribution to sustainable development (Tenuta, 2009).

Each firm should identify the ideal level of CSR that managers can determine through a cost-benefit analysis, thus avoiding high costs that do not generate subsequent revenues for the company and, therefore, a negative effect on performance (McWilliams & Siegel, 2001).

CSR helps achieve sustainability (Moon, 2007; Fisher et al., 2009) as they have been implemented to make society carbon neutral (Dey et al., 2020). CSR and corporate sustainability are intertwined (Montiel, 2008) and evidently, "The financial and economic crises imposed a reinterpretation of economic, managerial, and social sciences in an ethical key" (Gatto, 2020).

Therefore, the concept of CSR is interconnected with that of sustainable development since social responsibility is nothing more than the contribution that companies make to sustainable development.

## 3 Sustainability and Sustainable Development

Over the years, the concept of sustainable development has been the subject of growing interest from civil society (Waas et al., 2011). It results from a greater awareness of the exhaustion of the planet's resources and of the increasingly pressing need to preserve the quality of the natural heritage, aiming to promote more balanced economic and social development models than those adopted in the past. It is immediately evident that one of the characterizing aspects of sustainable development is the multidisciplinary approach: it combines environmental, economic, and social problems (Seuring & Gold, 2013). This type of approach, also known as the triple bottom line, was proposed by the World Commission on Environment and Development, which bases its vision of sustainable development precisely on the analysis of the three dimensions: economic, social, and environmental. Development is defined as sustainable if it can generate a substantial balance between the three areas: social, economic, environmental or if the so-called rule of the balance of the three "E" is valid: ecology, equity, economy. Therefore, an organization is stable not only financially but when it minimizes its negative environmental impacts and acts in consideration of the need to address future generations with an attitude of greater responsibility regarding what is produced not only in economic terms but also in ethical, environmental, and social terms (Chirieleison, 2002). If up to a certain point ethics was related only to relationships between contemporaries, from a certain point onwards, we begin to reflect on the behavior that a generation must have towards another (Tenuta, 2009).

Regulatory principles and guidelines have grown significantly over the years. A large number of codes and guidelines focused on some fundamental standards, such as the Sustainability Reporting Guidelines of the Global Reporting Initiative, the United Nations Global Compact and the Sustainable Development Goals, the Greenhouse Gas Protocol of the World Resources Institute and the Principles United Nations for Responsible Investment (Camilleri, 2017).

The focus on sustainable development allows organizations to reduce costs, increase both the rate of innovation and profitability, and improve efficiency (Magadza, 2000). Obviously, it is not enough to proclaim oneself sustainable. The emphasis on "sustainable development" minimizes its credibility by becoming a label for unsustainable and undeveloped ways (Luke, 2005). Kollmuss and Agyeman (2002) define the knowledge-behavior gap as the difference between the rhetoric of sustainability and sustainable behavior.

## 4 Corporate Sustainability

Leading businesses towards sustainability require a change in conceiving and measuring one's performance. To do this, it is necessary to think in terms of triple bottom lines, i.e., to adopt management methods aimed at jointly maximizing the three economic, social, and environmental dimensions (Eccles & Krzus, 2010). The three dimensions present a trade-off that the firm must consider in making ethically good decisions (Elkington, 1997).

In the past, sustainability has usually been linked to the environment (Funk, 2003). According to Montiel (2008), there are two very different ways of defining and conceptualizing CS. One approach uses the term ecological sustainability to identify CS primarily with the environmental dimension of the business (Starik & Rands, 1995). Other scholars follow the WCED definition and identify CS in its three-dimensional approach, including the economic, social, and environmental spheres (Bansal, 2005; Gladwin & Kennelly, 1995).

The economic bottom line of a company that indicates the operating profit and its performance is measured by recording a series of numerical data. Underlying it is the concept of economic capital as the total value of assets net of liabilities. However, we must not forget the intangible factors, one of the primary sources of competitive advantage in today's company (Rusconi & Dorigatti, 2004).

To address the issue of the social bottom line, it is necessary to define social capital, understood as the ability of people to work together for common purposes within groups and/or organizations, which is based on the acquisition and maintenance of values such as loyalty, honesty, and reliability (Fukujama, 1995). As part of the company, the company cannot exempt itself from behaving responsibly towards the whole range of stakeholders with which it relates.

On environmental issues, the interest of organizations dated back to the early seventies and emerged to report on the environmental impact of the activity carried out. It is necessary to operate according to environmental standards of reference, allowing a subsequent verification activity to be carried out.

According to Le Breton-Miller and Miller (2016), the literature on sustainability and CSR has been increasing for several years now due to the negative impacts of unsustainable business practices and has probably been amplified by the corporate underworld demonstrated by the recent financial crisis.

In fact, the first definition of "sustainability" is contained in the Report Our Common Future drawn up in 1987 by the World Commission on Environment and Development (Bruntland Commission). Sustainable development is defined as "guaranteeing the needs of current generations without compromising the possibility that future generations will be able to satisfy their own" (Tenuta, 2009). do Prado et al. (2020) point out that this definition is helpful in general terms but does not provide a detail of the development of sustainable practices and their application to businesses. For this reason, the intervention of numerous authors has been aimed at filling this gap through various definitions.

An application of this definition is provided by Dyllick and Hockerts (2002), who state that sustainability can be defined as the ability to meet the needs of the current stakeholders of a company without compromising its ability to satisfy the needs of future stakeholders. The authors argue that businesses must "maintain their economic, social, and environmental capital base."

Similarly, Kurapatskie and Darnall (2013) define CS as the ability of a company to reduce or eliminate its impact on the environment by satisfying the needs of its current and future stakeholders.

CS is defined as a corporate approach that creates long-term value for shareholders by looking at the economic, environmental, and social dimensions (Dow Jones Sustainability Indexes, 2019). According to Kok et al. (2019), CS is identified in the ability of a company to balance social, economic, and environmental objectives. Hahn et al. (2015) believe that CS presupposes an integrated vision of economic, environmental, and social aspects in a very similar way. The authors pause to specify that the search for the triple bottom line approach should be balanced without emphasizing one aspect over the other.

## 5 Circular Economy and Sustainability

The idea of a circular economy (CE) can be traced back to the 1920s (Leontief, 1928, 1991). Since then, the need for circular systems within the global economy to ensure long-term life has become increasingly evident (Boulding, 1966). For a long time, we have used the logic of linear economics, which, based on an industrial mentality, produces negative impacts on the environment, the economy, and society (Ellen MacArthur Foundation 2013). It becomes clear that the traditional linear economy cannot be sustainable, so a circular system is needed (Pearce & Turner, 1989). However, reuse has only recently been intended as a solution for a sustainable future (Ki et al., 2020) and numerous research has emerged through which scholars have fueled the debate on CE (McDowall et al., 2017).

Individual countries, encouraged in various ways, have worked towards a transition to the CE on the world stage. For instance, the European Commission (2015) argued that "the transition to a more circular economy, in which the value of products, materials, and resources is maintained in the economy for as long as possible and the production of waste is minimized, is an essential contribution to the European Union's efforts to develop a sustainable, low-carbon, resource-efficient and competitive economy." The World Business Council for Sustainable Development (2017) stated that "by moving towards the circular economy, countries and businesses can reap greater growth; innovation and competitive advantage, while enjoying cost savings; reduction of energy use and CO2 emissions, as well as a better supply chain and resource security."

On this basis, several countries have introduced national strategies that aim to achieve a more circular economy (Jones & Comfort, 2017). China, for example, introduced the CE as a new development strategy in 2002 and enacted the Circular Economy Promotion Law in 2009 (Geng et al., 2012). In Europe, a Circular Economy Action Plan was established in 2015 with a financial support package of over €6 billion.

Although there is no shared definition of CE in the literature, the idea is shared that in the CE model the products and materials are kept in a circle for as long as possible, they do not die after their primary use but are transformed into a second life (Puntillo et al., 2021).

After examining 114 definitions by various authors, Kirchherr et al. (2017) described the CE as an economic system in which the concept of "end of life" is replaced through reduction, reuse, and recycling. Several authors consider the CE to be an ethical approach based on the 3R principle "Reduce, reuse and recycle" (Qiao & Qiao, 2013; Murray et al., 2017; Wang et al., 2014). Geisendorf and Pietrulla (2018) propose a definition according to which "in a circular economy, the value of products and materials is maintained, waste is avoided, and resources are kept within the economy when a product has reached end of his life."

The analysis of the link between the CE and sustainability is widespread in the literature (Korhonen et al., 2018). The CE is considered vital for sustainable development (Ghisellini et al., 2016). Numerous researchers believe that the CE can increase resource productivity and overcome global sustainability challenges (Khan et al., 2020). Millar et al. (2019) believe that the CE approach is central in the debate on sustainability policy to realize the three dimensions of sustainable development. For Antikainen and Valkokari (2016), the CE contributes to sustainable economic growth and global competitiveness. Martins (2016) argues that understanding ecosystem services and sustainability can be achieved through the CE model. Murray et al. (2017) argue that it is possible to balance economic development with protecting the environment and resources through the CE. Geissdoerfer et al. (2017), Prieto-Sandoval et al. (2018), and Kirchherr et al. (2017) define the CE as an essential element to achieving sustainability to be pursued at the micro- and macro-level. De Jesus and Mendonça (2018) consider the CE as a multidimensional approach that has as its final goal the economic development in a sustainable way. Schroeder et al. (2019) carried out an analysis in order to identify the extent to which circular economy (CE) practices are essential for the implementation of the Sustainable Development Goals (SDGs), demonstrating that "CE practices can potentially be used directly to achieve a significant number of SDG objectives."

Another line of research analyzes the impact of the CE and its possible economic benefits. CE scholars are interested in how waste management and recycling generate economic value (Betancourt Morales & Zartha Sossa, 2020). Numerous scholars and professionals observe that the EC can incentivize companies' sustainable competitive advantage. CE is a key strategy for achieving corporate sustainability (Ghisellini et al., 2016; Murray et al., 2017). It represents the essential component for companies seeking a sustainable approach (Reif & Rexhäuser, 2018), looking at the economic, social, and environmental fields simultaneously. Organizations adopt the CE trying to make their operations sustainable from an environmental point of view and at the same time obtain economic benefits (Ghisellini et al., 2016). Therefore, through the CE, an attempt is made to balance environmental and economic objectives (Centobelli et al., 2020; Saidani et al., 2019). Achieve economic objectives without impacting the environment (Zhu et al., 2010). According to Aboulamer (2018), the CE produces positive externalities that translate into financial gain for shareholders.

Furthermore, investors tend to penalize companies that do not adopt a corporate sustainability strategy (Lourenço et al., 2012). According to Horbach and Rammer (2019), the CE positively impacts businesses mainly in terms of cost reduction and increased competitiveness. In their econometric analysis, the authors find that companies implementing CE innovations experience higher sales and employment growth than other companies in the same industry.

Therefore, it would seem clear that it is possible to reduce raw materials through more efficient production, which creates a win-win situation for all from an environmental and economic point of view (Van der Byl & Slawinski, 2015). A win-win situation is the most frequently encountered empirical case in the CE context (Daddi et al., 2019). Numerous studies believe that the CE could produce significant cost savings, job creation, innovation, productivity, and resource efficiency (Gower & Schroeder, 2016). The CE "would allow Europe to increase resource productivity by up to 3% per year" and could generate a net economic benefit of €1.8 trillion by 2030 (Jones & Comfort, 2017).

The CE has gained increasing attention (Lieder & Rashid, 2016). "The transition to a circular economy is a step towards sustainability." High levels of corporate sustainability create a competitive advantage that translates into an economic advantage for shareholders (Aboulamer, 2018). Companies have understood the need to include environmental, social, and economic sustainability within the different management models (Buxel et al., 2015), which necessarily passes through the implementation of the CE. The resulting benefits can be internal, external, or both (Orlitzky et al., 2003). Possible positive effects relate to employee motivation, morale, and commitment to work (Brammer et al., 2007). The external advantages concern the impact on corporate reputation (Gallego-Álvarez et al., 2010; Hussainey & Salama, 2010).

## References

Aboulamer, A. (2018). Adopting a circular business model improves market equity value. *Thunderbird International Business Review, 60*(5), 765–769. https://doi.org/10.1002/tie.21922

Allen, W. (2001). The mysterious art of corporate governance. *Corporate Board, 22*, 1–5.

Antikainen, M., & Valkokari, K. (2016). A framework for sustainable circular business model innovation. *Technology Innovation Management Review, 6*(7). www.timreview.ca

Bandettini, A. (1981). *Responsabilità sociale dell'impresa, in Bilancio d'esercizio e amministrazione delle imprese. Studi in onore di Pietro Onida* (pp. 333–353). Giuffrè.

Bansal, P. (2005). Evolving sustainably: A longitudinal study of corporate sustainable development. *Strategic Management Journal, 26*(3), 197–218. https://doi.org/10.1002/smj.441

Bartocci, L. (2003). *Il bilancio sociale negli enti locali. Fondamenti teorici e aspetti metodologici*. Giappichelli.

Beda, A., & Bodo, R. (2006). *La responsabilità sociale d'impresa. Strumenti e strategie per uno sviluppo sostenibile dell'economia*. Il Sole 24 Ore.

Bertoli, S. (2007). *Il mestiere di CSR manager. Politiche di responsabilità sociale nelle imprese italiane*. Il Sole 24 Ore.

Betancourt Morales, C. M., & Zartha Sossa, J. W. (2020). Circular economy in Latin America: A systematic literature review. *Business Strategy and the Environment, 29*(6), 2479–2497. https://doi.org/10.1002/bse.2515

Birindelli, G., & Taraballa, A. (2001). *La responsabilità sociale delle imprese e i nuovi strumenti di comunicazione nell'esperienza bancaria italiana*. FrancoAngeli.

Borgonovi, E., Aiello, G., & Fellegara, A. M. (2017). *Sviluppo, sostenibilità e competitività delle aziende. Il contributo degli economisti aziendali*. Il Mulino.

Borgonovi, E., & Rusconi, G. (2008). *La responsabilità sociale delle istituzioni di pubblico interesse*. FrancoAngeli.

Boulding, K. E. (1966). The economics of the coming spaceship earth. In H. Jarrett (Ed.), *Environmental quality issues in a growing economy* (pp. 3–14). Johns Hopkins University Press.

Bowen, H. R. (2013). *Social responsibilities of the businessman*. University of Iowa Press.

Bowie, N. (1995). New direction in corporate social responsibility. In W. M. Hoffman & R. E. Frederick (Eds.), *Business ethics–readings and cases in corporate morality*. McGraw-Hill.

Brammer, S., Millington, A., & Rayton, B. (2007). The contribution of corporate social responsibility to organizational commitment. *International Journal of Human Resource Management, 18*(10), 1701–1719. https://doi.org/10.1080/09585190701570866

Brunk, K. H. (2012). Un/ethical company and brand perceptions: Conceptualising and Operationalising consumer meanings. *Journal of Business Ethics, 111*(4), 551–565. https://doi.org/10.1007/s10551-012-1339-x

Bufera, F., & Catino, M. (2002). L'impresa eccellente socialmente capace. *Impresa e Stato, 58.*

Burke, L., & Logsdon, J. M. (1996). How corporate social responsibility pays off. *Long Range Planning, 29*(4), 495–502. https://doi.org/10.1016/0024-6301(96)00041-6

Buxel, H., Esenduran, G., & Griffin, S. (2015). Strategic sustainability: Creating business value with life cycle analysis. *Business Horizons, 58*(1), 109–122. https://doi.org/10.1016/j.bushor.2014.09.004

Camilleri, M. A. (2017). Corporate sustainability and responsibility: Creating value for business, society and the environment. *Asian Journal of Sustainability and Social Responsibility, 2*(1), 59–74. https://doi.org/10.1186/s41180-017-0016-5

Campedelli, B. (2005). *Reporting aziendale e sostenibilità. I nuovi orizzonti del bilancio sociale.* FrancoAngeli.

Carnevale, C., & Carnevale, V. (2008). *Comunicare la sostenibilità. Strumenti informativi e di reporting nelle regioni italiane*. FrancoAngeli.

Carnevale, C. (2005). *L'informazione etico-sociale nella comunicazione d'impresa*. FrancoAngeli.

Carroll, A. B. (1999). Corporate social responsibility: Evolution of a definitional construct. *Business and Society, 38*(3), 268–295. https://doi.org/10.1177/000765039903800303

Cassidy, D. (2003). Maximizing shareholder value: The risks to employees, customers and the community. *Corporate Governance: The International Journal of Business in Society, 3*(2), 32–37. https://doi.org/10.1108/14720700310474046

Catturi, G. (2003). *Valori etici e principi economici: equilibrio possibile*. Stamperia dell'Università di Siena.

Cavalieri, E. (1981). Aspetti sociali dell'informazione economica d'impresa. *Rivista italiana di Ragioneria e di Economia Aziendale, 3*, 108–120.

Cavalieri, E. (2002). *Economia ed Etica aziendale*. Giappichelli.

Cavicchi, P. (2003). *Bilancio sociale e ambientale. Responsabilità sociale e ambientale dell'impresa*. Ipsoa.

Centobelli, P., Cerchione, R., Chiaroni, D., Del Vecchio, P., & Urbinati, A. (2020). Designing business models in circular economy: A systematic literature review and research agenda. *Business Strategy and the Environment, 29*(4), 1734–1749. https://doi.org/10.1002/bse.2466

Chami, R., Cosimano, T. F., & Fullenkamp, C. (2002). Managing ethical risk: How investing in ethics adds value. *Journal of Banking and Finance, 26*(9), 1697–1718. https://doi.org/10.1016/S0378-4266(02)00188-7

Chirieleison, C. (2002). *Le strategie sociali nel governo dell'azienda*. Giuffrè.

Coda, V. (1996). *I codici etici nella gestione aziendale*. Il Sole 24 Ore.

Daddi, T., Ceglia, D., Bianchi, G., & de Barcellos, M. D. (2019). Paradoxical tensions and corporate sustainability: A focus on circular economy business cases. *Corporate Social Responsibility and Environmental Management, 26*(4), 770–780. https://doi.org/10.1002/csr.1719

Dalle, F., & Bounine, J. (1975). *Quand l'entreprise s' éveille à la conscience sociale*. R. Laffont.

de Jesus, A., & Mendonça, S. (2018). Lost in transition? Drivers and barriers in the eco-innovation road to the circular economy. *Ecological Economics, 145*, 75–89. https://doi.org/10.1016/j.ecolecon.2017.08.001

De Waegeneer, E., Van De Sompele, J., & Willem, A. (2016). Ethical codes in sports organizations: Classification framework, content analysis, and the influence of content on code effectiveness. *Journal of Business Ethics, 136*(3), 587–598. https://doi.org/10.1007/s10551-014-2531-y

Dey, P. K., Malesios, C., De, D., Budhwar, P., Chowdhury, S., & Cheffi, W. (2020). Circular economy to enhance sustainability of small and medium-sized enterprises. *Business Strategy and the Environment, 29*(6), 2145–2169. https://doi.org/10.1002/bse.2492

Diez-Cañamero, B., Bishara, T., Otegi-Olaso, J. R., Minguez, R., & Fernández, J. M. (2020). Measurement of corporate social responsibility: A review of corporate sustainability indexes, rankings and ratings. *Sustainability, 12*(5). https://doi.org/10.3390/su12052153

do Prado, G. F., Piekarski, C. M., da Luz, L. M., de Souza, J. T., Salvador, R., & de Francisco, A. C. (2020). Sustainable development and economic performance: Gaps and trends for future research. *Sustainable Development, 28*(1), 368–384. https://doi.org/10.1002/sd.1982

Donaldson, T., & Preston, L. E. (1995). The stakeholder theory of the corporation: Concepts, evidence, and implications. *Academy of Management Review, 20*, 65–91. https://doi.org/10.5465/amr.1995.9503271992

Dyllick, T., & Hockerts, K. (2002). Beyond the business case for corporate sustainability. *Business Strategy and the Environment, 11*(2), 130–141. https://doi.org/10.1002/bse.323

Eccles, R. G., & Krzus, M. P. (2010). *One report: Integrated reporting for a sustainable strategy*. John Wiley & Sons.

Elkington, J. (1997). *Cannibals with forks: The triple bottom line of 21st century business*. Capstone.

Ferrell, O. C., Harrison, D. E., Ferrell, L., & Hair, J. F. (2019). Business ethics, corporate social responsibility, and brand attitudes: An exploratory study. *Journal of Business Research, 95*, 491–501. https://doi.org/10.1016/j.jbusres.2018.07.039

Fisher, K., Geenen, J., Jurcevic, M., McClintock, K., & Davis, G. (2009). Applying asset-based community development as a strategy for CSR: A Canadian perspective on a win-win for stakeholders and SMEs. *Business Ethics: A European Review, 18*(1), 66–82. https://doi.org/10.1111/j.1467-8608.2009.01549.x

Frederick, W. C. (1960). The growing concern over business responsibility. *California Management Review, 2*(4), 54–61. https://doi.org/10.2307/41165405

Frederick, W. C. (1986). Toward CSR3 why ethical analysis is indispensable and unavoidable in corporate affairs. *Californian Management Review, 28*, 126–141.

Frederick, W. C. (1994). From CSR to CRS. *Business & Society, 33*(2), 150–164.

Freeman, R. E. (1984). *Strategic management. A stakeholder approach*. Pitman.

Friedman, M. (1962). *Capitalism and freedom*. University of Chicago Press.

Friedman, M. (1970). *The social responsibility of business is to increase its profits*. New York Times Magazine.

Fukujama, F. (1995). *Trust: The social virtues and the creation of prosperity*. Free Press.

Funk, K. (2003). Sustainability and performance. *MIT Sloan Management Review, 44*(2), 65–70.

Gabrovec Mei, O. (2002). *Bilancio sociale e valore aggiunto, in Hinna, L. Il bilancio sociale*. Il Sole 24 Ore.

Gagliardi, P. (1995). *Le imprese come culture: nuove prospettive di analisi organizzative*. Isedi.

Gallego-Álvarez, I., Prado-Lorenzo, J. M., Rodríguez-Domínguez, L., & García-Sánchez, I. M. (2010). Are social and environmental practices a marketing tool?: Empirical evidence for the biggest European companies. *Management Decision, 48*(10), 1440–1455. https://doi.org/10.1108/00251741011090261

Gatto, A. (2020). A pluralistic approach to economic and business sustainability: A critical meta-synthesis of foundations, metrics, and evidence of human and local development. *Corporate Social Responsibility and Environmental Management, 27*(4), 1525–1539. https://doi.org/10.1002/csr.1912

Geisendorf, S., & Pietrulla, F. (2018). The circular economy and circular economic concepts—A literature analysis and redefinition. *Thunderbird International Business Review, 60*(5), 771–782. https://doi.org/10.1002/tie.21924

Geissdoerfer, M., Savaget, P., Bocken, N. M. P., & Hultink, E. J. (2017). The circular economy–a new sustainability paradigm? *Journal of Cleaner Production, 143*, 757–768. Elsevier Ltd. https://doi.org/10.1016/j.jclepro.2016.12.048

Geng, Y., Fu, J., Sarkis, J., & Xue, B. (2012). Towards a national circular economy indicator system in China: An evaluation and critical analysis. *Journal of Cleaner Production, 23*(1), 216–224. https://doi.org/10.1016/j.jclepro.2011.07.005

Ghisellini, P., Cialani, C., & Ulgiati, S. (2016). A review on circular economy: The expected transition to a balanced interplay of environmental and economic systems. *Journal of Cleaner Production, 114*, 11–32. https://doi.org/10.1016/j.jclepro.2015.09.007

Gladwin, T. N., & Kennelly, J. J. (1995). Shifting paradigms for sustainable development: Implications for management theory and research. *Academy of Management Review, 20*(4), 874–907. https://doi.org/10.5465/amr.1995.9512280024

Gower, R., & Schroeder, P. (2016). *Virtuous circle: How the circular economy can save lives and create jobs in low and middle income countries*. Tearfund and Institute of Development Studies.

Gray, R., Adams, C., & Owen, D. (1996). *Accounting and accountability: Changes and challenge in corporate social and environmental reporting*. Prentice Hall International.

Hahn, T., Pinkse, J., Preuss, L., & Figge, F. (2015). Tensions in corporate sustainability: Towards an integrative framework. *Journal of Business Ethics, 127*(2), 297–316. https://doi.org/10.1007/s10551-014-2047-5

Helin, S., & Sandström, J. (2007). An inquiry into the study of corporate codes of ethics. *Journal of Business Ethics, 75*(3), 253–271. https://doi.org/10.1007/s10551-006-9251-x

Hinna, L. (2005). *Come gestire la responsabilità sociale dell'impresa*. Il Sole 24 ore.

Horbach, J., & Rammer, C. (2019). Employment and performance effects of circular economy innovations. *SSRN Electronic Journal, 19-016*(05), 1–20. https://doi.org/10.2139/ssrn.3383936

Hussainey, K., & Salama, A. (2010). The importance of corporate environmental reputation to investors. *Journal of Applied Accounting Research, 11*(3), 229–241. https://doi.org/10.1108/09675421011088152

Joner, B. E., & Payne, D. (2002). Evolution and implementation: A study of values, business ethics and corporate social responsibility. *Journal of Business Ethics, 41*, 297–311.

Jones, P., & Comfort, D. (2017). Towards the circular economy: A commentary on corporate approaches and challenges. *Journal of Public Affairs, 17*(4), 1–5. https://doi.org/10.1002/pa.1680

Kaptein, M., & Schwartz, M. S. (2008). The effectiveness of business codes: A critical examination of existing studies and the development of an integrated research model. *Journal of Business Ethics, 77*(2), 111–127. https://doi.org/10.1007/s10551-006-9305-0

Khan, O., Daddi, T., & Iraldo, F. (2020). The role of dynamic capabilities in circular economy implementation and performance of companies. *Corporate Social Responsibility and Environmental Management, 27*(6), 3018–3033. https://doi.org/10.1002/csr.2020

Ki, C. W., Chong, S. M., & Ha-Brookshire, J. E. (2020). How fashion can achieve sustainable development through a circular economy and stakeholder engagement: A systematic literature review. *Corporate Social Responsibility and Environmental Management, 27*(6), 2401–2424. https://doi.org/10.1002/csr.1970

Kirchherr, J., Reike, D., & Hekkert, M. (2017). Conceptualizing the circular economy: An analysis of 114 definitions. *Resources, Conservation and Recycling, 127*, 221–232. https://doi.org/10.1016/j.resconrec.2017.09.005

Kok, A. M., de Bakker, F. G. A., & Groenewegen, P. (2019). Sustainability struggles: Conflicting cultures and incompatible logics. *Business and Society, 58*(8), 1496–1532. https://doi.org/10.1177/0007650317703644

Kollmuss, A., & Agyeman, J. (2002). Mind the gap: Why do people act environmentally and what are the barriers to pro-environmental behavior? *Environmental Education Research, 8*(3), 239–260. https://doi.org/10.1080/13504620220145401

Korhonen, J., Nuur, C., Feldmann, A., & Birkie, S. E. (2018). Circular economy as an essentially contested concept. *Journal of Cleaner Production, 175*, 544–552. https://doi.org/10.1016/j.jclepro.2017.12.111

Kurapatskie, B., & Darnall, N. (2013). Which corporate sustainability activities are associated with greater financial payoffs? *Business Strategy and the Environment, 22*(1), 49–61. https://doi.org/10.1002/bse.1735

Lantos, G. P. (2001). The boundaries of strategic corporate social responsibility. *Journal of Consumer Marketing, 18*(7), 595–632. https://doi.org/10.1108/07363760110410281

Latapí Agudelo, M. A., Jóhannsdóttir, L., & Davídsdóttir, B. (2019). A literature review of the history and evolution of corporate social responsibility. *Int J Corporate Soc Responsibility, 4*(1). https://doi.org/10.1186/s40991-018-0039-y

Le Breton-Miller, I., & Miller, D. (2016). Family firms and practices of sustainability: A contingency view. *Journal of Family Business Strategy, 7*(1), 26–33. https://doi.org/10.1016/j.jfbs.2015.09.001

Leontief, W. (1928). Die Wirtschaft als Kreislauf. *Archiv für Sozialwissenschaft und Sozialpolitik, 60*(3), 577–623.

Leontief, W. (1991). The economy as a circular flow. *Structural Change and Economic Dynamics, 2*(1), 181–212. https://doi.org/10.1016/0954-349X(91)90012-H

Levitt, T. (1958). The dangers of social-responsibility. *Harvard Business Review, 36*(5), 41–50.

Lieder, M., & Rashid, A. (2016). Towards circular economy implementation: A comprehensive review in context of manufacturing industry. *Journal of Cleaner Production, 115*, 36–51. Elsevier Ltd. https://doi.org/10.1016/j.jclepro.2015.12.042

Lo, S. F., & Sheu, H. J. (2007). Is corporate sustainability a value-increasing strategy for business? *Corporate Governance: An International Review, 15*(2), 345–358. https://doi.org/10.1111/j.1467-8683.2007.00565.x

Lourenço, I. C., Branco, M. C., Curto, J. D., & Eugénio, T. (2012). How does the market value corporate sustainability performance? *Journal of Business Ethics, 108*(4), 417–428. https://doi.org/10.1007/s10551-011-1102-8

Luke, T. W. (2005). Neither sustainable nor development: Reconsidering sustainability in development. *Sustainable Development, 13*(4), 228–238. https://doi.org/10.1002/sd.284

Magadza, C. H. D. (2000). Climate change impacts and human settlements in Africa: Prospects for adaptation. *Environmental Monitoring and Assessment, 61*, 193–205.

Martins, N. O. (2016). Ecosystems, strong sustainability and the classical circular economy. *Ecological Economics, 129*, 32–39. https://doi.org/10.1016/j.ecolecon.2016.06.003

Matacena, A. (1984). *Impresa e ambiente. Il «bilancio sociale»*. Clueb.

Mazzoleni, M. (2006). Impresa e responsabilità sociale. In G. Rusconi & M. Dorigatti (Eds.), *Imprese e Società*. FrancoAngeli.

McDowall, W., Geng, Y., Huang, B., Barteková, E., Bleischwitz, R., Türkeli, S., Kemp, R., & Doménech, T. (2017). Circular economy policies in China and Europe. *Journal of Industrial Ecology, 21*(3), 651–661. https://doi.org/10.1111/jiec.12597

McGuire, J. W. (1963). *Business and society*. McGraw-hill.

McWilliams, A., & Siegel, D. (2001). Corporate social responsibility: A theory of the firm perspective. *Academy of Management Review, 26*(1). https://doi.org/10.5465/amr.2001.4011987

Millar, N., McLaughlin, E., & Börger, T. (2019). The circular economy: Swings and roundabouts? *Ecological Economics, 158*, 11–19. https://doi.org/10.1016/j.ecolecon.2018.12.012

Mintzberg, H. (1983). The case for corporate social responsibility. *Journal of Business Strategy, 4*(2), 3–15. https://doi.org/10.1108/eb039015

Molteni, M. (2004). *Responsabilità sociale e performance d'impresa*. Vita e pensiero.

Montiel, I. (2008). Corporate social responsibility and corporate sustainability: Separate pasts, common futures. *Organization and Environment, 21*(3), 245–269. https://doi.org/10.1177/1086026608321329

Moon, J. (2007). The contribution of corporate social responsibility to sustainable development. *Sustainable Development, 15*(5), 296–306. https://doi.org/10.1002/sd.346

Murray, A., Skene, K., & Haynes, K. (2017). The circular economy: An interdisciplinary exploration of the concept and application in a global context. *Journal of Business Ethics, 140*(3), 369–380. https://doi.org/10.1007/s10551-015-2693-2

Mussari, R., & Monfardini, P. (2010). Practices of social reporting in public sector and non profit organizations. *Public Management Review, 12*(4).

Orlitzky, M., Schmidt, F. L., & Rynes, S. L. (2003). Corporate social and financial performance: A meta-analysis. *Organization Studies, 24*(3), 403–441. https://doi.org/10.1177/0170840603024003910

Orlitzky, M., Siegel, D. S., & Waldman, D. A. (2011). Strategic corporate social responsibility and environmental sustainability. *Business and Society, 50*(1), 6–27. https://doi.org/10.1177/0007650310394323

Pae, J., & Choi, T. H. (2011). Corporate governance, commitment to business ethics, and firm valuation: Evidence from the Korean stock market. *Journal of Business Ethics, 100*(2), 323–348. https://doi.org/10.1007/s10551-010-0682-z

Pearce, D. W., & Turner, R. K. (1989). *Economics of natural resources and the environment*. Johns Hopkins University Press.

Porter, M. E., & Kramer, R. M. (2006). The link between competitive advantage and corporate social responsibility. *Harvard Business Review, 84*(12), 78–92.

Prieto-Sandoval, V., Jaca, C., & Ormazabal, M. (2018). Towards a consensus on the circular economy. *Journal of Cleaner Production, 179*, 605–615. https://doi.org/10.1016/j.jclepro.2017.12.224

Pulejo, A. (1996). *Esperienze in tema di bilancio sociale: il modello francese*. Giappichelli.

Puntillo, P., Gulluscio, C., Huisingh, D., & Veltri, S. (2021). Reevaluating waste as a resource under a circular economy approach from a system perspective: Findings from a case study. *Business Strategy and the Environment, 30*(2), 968–984. https://doi.org/10.1002/bse.2664

Qiao, F., & Qiao, N. (2013). Circular economy: An ethical and sustainable economic development model. *Prakseologia, 154*, 253–272.

Rapport, A. (1989). *La strategia del valore: le nuove regole della performance aziendale*. FrancoAngeli.

Reif, C., & Rexhäuser, S. (2018). Good enough! Are socially responsible companies the more successful environmental innovators? In J. Horbach & C. Reif (Eds.), *New developments in eco-innovation research. Sustainability and innovation*. Springer. https://doi.org/10.1007/978-3-319-93019-0_8

Reinhardt, F. L. (2017). Market failure and the environmental policies of firms: Economic rationales for "beyond compliance" behavior. *Corporate Environmental Responsibility, 3*(1), 171–183. http://www.people.hbs.edu/freinhardt/bio.html

Ricci, P. (2010). L'art.41 della Costituzione Italiana e la responsabilità sociale d'impresa. *Rivista Italiana di Ragioneria e di Economia Aziendale, 3-4*, 142–150.

Rija, M., & Tenuta, P. (2010). *L'etica e la responsabilità sociale delle imprese nella teoria e nel business reale*. FrancoAngeli.

Rusconi, G. (1988). *Il bilancio sociale d'impresa. Problemi e prospettive*. Giuffrè.

Rusconi, G., & Dorigatti, M. (2004). *La responsabilità sociale d'impresa*. Fondazione Acli Milanesi.

Sacconi, L., & Baldin, E. (2003). Come le organizzazioni possono essere socialmente responsabili? *Sviluppo & Organizzazione, 186*.

Saidani, M., Yannou, B., Leroy, Y., Cluzel, F., & Kendall, A. (2019). A taxonomy of circular economy indicators. *Journal of Cleaner Production, 207*, 542–559. https://doi.org/10.1016/j.jclepro.2018.10.014

Saygili, E. E., & Öztürkoğlu, Y. (2017). Corporate governance and social responsibility issues in code of ethics. *Haziran, 19*(2), 378–388. https://dergipark.org.tr/en/pub/mbdd/issue/54663/745942

Schroeder, P., Anggraeni, K., & Weber, U. (2019). The relevance of circular economy practices to the sustainable development goals. *Journal of Industrial Ecology, 23*(1), 77–95. https://doi.org/10.1111/jiec.12732

Schwartz, M. S., & Carroll, A. B. (2008). Integrating and unifying competing and complementary frameworks: The search for a common core in the business and society field. *Business and Society, 47*(2), 148–186. https://doi.org/10.1177/0007650306297942

Sen, S., Bhattacharya, C. B., & Korschun, D. (2006). The role of corporate social responsibility in strengthening multiple stakeholder relationships: A field experiment. *Journal of the Academy of Marketing Science, 34*(2), 158–166. https://doi.org/10.1177/0092070305284978

Seuring, S., & Gold, S. (2013). Sustainability management beyond corporate boundaries: From stakeholders to performance. *Journal of Cleaner Production, 56*, 1–6. https://doi.org/10.1016/j.jclepro.2012.11.033

Singh, J. B. (2011). Determinants of the effectiveness of corporate codes of ethics: An empirical study. *Journal of Business Ethics, 101*(3), 385–395. https://doi.org/10.1007/s10551-010-0727-3

Smith, A. (1759). In A. Millar, A. Kincaid, J. Bell, & A. M. Kelley (Eds.), *The theory of moral sentiments*. Originally published.

Starik, M., & Rands, G. P. (1995). Weaving an integrated web: Multilevel and multisystem perspectives of ecologically sustainable organizations. *Academy of Management Review, 20*(4). https://doi.org/10.5465/amr.1995.9512280025

Tenuta, P. (2009). *Indici e modelli di sostenibilità*. FrancoAngeli.

Terzani, S. (1984). Responsabilità sociale dell'azienda. *Rivista Italiana di Ragioneria e di Economia Aziendale, 7-8*, 286–299.

Van der Byl, C. A., & Slawinski, N. (2015). Embracing tensions in corporate sustainability: A review of research from win-wins and trade-offs to paradoxes and beyond. *Organization and Environment, 28*(1), 54–79. https://doi.org/10.1177/1086026615575047

van Marrewijk, M., & Werre, M. (2003). Multiple levels of corporate sustainability. *Journal of Business Ethics, 44*(2–3), 107–119. https://doi.org/10.1023/A:1023383229086

Viviani, M. (2006). *Dire, fare, dare, avere. Percorsi e pratiche di responsabilità sociale*. Il Mulino.

Waas, T., Hugé, J., Verbruggen, A., & Wright, T. (2011). Sustainable development: A bird's eye view. *Sustainability, 3*(10), 1637–1661. https://doi.org/10.3390/su3101637

Walton, C. C. (1982). Corporate social responsibility: The debate revisited. *Journal of Economics and Business, 34*, 173–187. https://doi.org/10.1016/0148-6195(82)90032-7

Wang, P. C., Che, F., Fan, S. S., & Gu, C. (2014). Ownership governance, institutional pressures and circular economy accounting information disclosure: An institutional theory and corporate governance theory perspective. *Chinese Management Studies, 8*(3), 487–501. https://doi.org/10.1108/CMS-10-2013-0192

Webley, S., & Werner, A. (2008). Corporate codes of ethics: Necessary but not sufficient. *Business Ethics: A European Review, 17*(4), 405–415. https://doi.org/10.1111/j.1467-8608.2008.00543.x

Zhu, Q., Geng, Y., Lai, K., & hung. (2010). Circular economy practices among Chinese manufacturers varying in environmental-oriented supply chain cooperation and the performance implications. *Journal of Environmental Management, 91*(6), 1324–1331. https://doi.org/10.1016/j.jenvman.2010.02.013

## References

[illegible]

# Chapter 3
# ESG Measures and Non-financial Performance Reporting

**Abstract** In the second chapter, we analyze the ways of measuring Corporate Sustainability (CS) and the evolution of social and environmental disclosure (SED) that have taken place from the 1970s to today. Sustainability is a multidimensional concept for which evaluating the performance of companies in terms of sustainability must take into account various ESG criteria. To this end, we use as a source of data the information provided on the official websites of ESG rating agencies, from previous scientific articles and the websites of the major companies present in the ratings and indexes analyzed to identify the prominent rating companies and the most widespread ESG indexes and facilitate companies and investors in selecting organizations. We provide a valuable review of the leading rating agencies' origins and the most popular ESG indexes.

We also examine the evolution of social and environmental disclosure (SED), which can be considered an example of corporate social and environmental sustainability.

Finally, we describe the Corporate Sustainability Reporting Directive (CSRD) 2021/0104, with which the European Commission sets itself the ultimate goal of bringing sustainability reporting to the same level as financial reporting.

The second chapter ends by indicating the first Exposure Drafts of standards relating to sustainability reporting by the International Sustainability Standards Board (ISSB).

## 1 Sustainability Indicators

In the literature, there are contradictory interpretations of the meaning of the term indicator (Gallopín, 1996). An indicator can be defined as a parameter, measure, model, metric, value, fraction, or sign. An indicator is a sign that requires interpretation (Jollands, 2006). Indicators that are typically identified as accurate representations, according to Moldan and Dahl (2012), instead of faithfully representing reality, are representations that can have varying degrees of accuracy.

Indicators should be used, comparable over time and space. An indicator is, in general, a measurement tool capable of providing a synthetic representation of the

© The Author(s), under exclusive license to Springer Nature Switzerland AG 2022 
P. Tenuta, D. R. Cambrea, *Corporate Sustainability*, SIDREA Series in Accounting and Business Administration, https://doi.org/10.1007/978-3-031-11491-5_3

phenomenon investigated to preserve the information content of the analysis. The OECD (Organization for Economic Co-operation and Development) defines an indicator as a parameter or value derived from parameters that indicate/provide information on the status of a phenomenon/scope/area with meaning beyond what is directly associated with the parameter's value. Furthermore, the term index is defined as a set of parameters, measurable or observable properties, or aggregated or weighted indicators (Tenuta, 2009).

Measuring sustainability requires the development of indicators (Reid & Rout, 2020). Recent trends have led to the need to measure, represent, and monitor sustainability through sets of indicators built to guide decision-making processes (Bell & Morse, 2008; Boggia, 2007). Several authors are critical of the validity of sustainability indicators (SI), particularly about the ability to enclose complex processes in a few measures that lead to values that are not always precise (Bell & Morse, 2008). Precisely, the consideration of enormously complex causal chains in the evaluation of sustainability presupposes the existence of unknowable and measurable socio-ecological systems (Stirling, 1999).

To assess sustainability, it is necessary to integrate indicators from different areas. The use of indicators allows:

- monitoring the evolution of a phenomenon by facilitating the comparison of data and orienting programming and planning choices towards more sustainable approaches and management models.
- facilitating the dissemination and communication to users of the results of the surveys (Gardini et al., 2003).

Therefore, measuring sustainability requires integrating the various aspects and opening up new methodological perspectives for the use of simple sectoral indicators. There are two distinct approaches:

- the identification of indicators and the elaboration of synthetic indexes, which bring together the complexity of sustainability in one or at least a few variables.
- the development of more or less extensive sets of indicators, including sectoral indicators.

Although the importance of the use of indicators is universally recognized, several open questions remain:

- the identification of adequate criteria for choosing the indicators.
- the definition of significant reference values and/or targets.
- the relationship between the indicators and the territorial, environmental, cultural, and social context in which the activity takes place.
- the collection and processing of data.

The definition of targets, threshold values, or reference levels that allow an assessment of the significance or trend towards sustainability is complex. In some cases, there are recognized threshold values; in other cases, it is necessary to consider the context in which one operates and the specific objectives to be achieved (Tenuta, 2009).

Numerous tools to encourage and measure the sustainable approach have been identified over the years. The Global Compact is an initiative launched at the World Economic Forum in 1999 to promote CSR and allow companies to contribute to sustainable development (Cetindamar, 2007). The nine universal principles became ten points to a more inclusive and sustainable global economy a few years later. At the same time, in 2000, the Millennium Summit was held in the USA. The United Nations Millennium Declaration was adopted in which a series of Millennium Development Goals (MDGs) were defined to be achieved by 2015. The Millennium Declaration defined 8 objectives, 18 targets, and 48 indicators that the states are committed to achieving and which are binding for the entire international community. In 2015, the 2030 Agenda for sustainable development was approved, the essential elements of which are 17 Sustainable Development Goals (SDGs), 169 sub-objectives, and 230 indicators, through which we seek to eliminate poverty and inequality and aim for global social and economic development. The SDGs are the successors of the MDGs, but their scope is much broader. New elements are introduced, such as climate change, economic inequality, innovation, and sustainable consumption (Sachs, 2012).

Among the various structural defects of the 2030 Agenda (Kumar et al., 2016), one of the best known and most important is that the objectives and indicators developed to monitor the implementation of the SDGs "have a macro-approach that makes their application difficult at the company level." For this reason, companies that have found themselves in difficulty in measuring their actual contribution to sustainable development have begun to use indexes and ratings that measure sustainability, very often expressed in environmental, social and governance (ESG) terms (Diez-Cañamero et al., 2020).

## 2 The ESG Rating

The sustainability performance of companies is essential for investors and other stakeholders (Hutton et al., 1998) because it informs them about the impact of management activities on sustainability (Papoutsi & Sodhi, 2020; Mahoney et al., 2013; Searcy, 2012). Sustainability is a multidimensional concept for which evaluating the performance of companies in terms of sustainability must take into account economic and non-economic (environmental, social and governance) criteria in an integrated way (Liern & Pérez-Gladish, 2018).

The request for accurate information from a financial point of view and an ESG point of view has become part of companies' competitive strategy This derives from the development of sustainable and responsible investment (SRI), which requires reliable data on the various companies' social, environmental, and governance performance (Hockerts & Moir, 2004).

The numerous ESG rating agencies that have sprung up in the last decade, and absorbed into the standard practice of financial rating agencies, are the result of this need (Avetisyan & Hockerts, 2017). This evolution has led ESG rating agencies, which evaluate corporate sustainability performance through their own methodologies, to be a key reference for companies, financial markets, and academia. For these reasons, ESG rating agencies bear a responsibility that goes beyond the scope of the financial markets, affecting society as a whole (Escrig-Olmedo et al., 2019). In fact, low ESG ratings can damage a company's reputation with its consequent effects. For example, KLD eliminated Coca-Cola Co. from its Broad Market Social Index in 2006 due to some unsustainable business practices in developing countries. This resulted in the sale of approximately $ 50 million of Coca-Cola Co. stock by the largest pension fund in the United States as well as fueling criticism of the company (Chatterji et al., 2009).

Trillions of dollars are invested based on ESG ratings, a trend that accelerated following the COVID-19 outbreak. As a result, ESG ratings may influence financial decisions, with potentially far-reaching implications for asset prices and corporate policies.

ESG ratings are often denominated differently. We commonly talk about CSR, social, sustainability, or SRI ratings (Avetisyan & Hockerts, 2017). In some cases, they are based on extra-financial information, while others combine financial and extra-financial data (Scalet & Kelly, 2010). Rating agencies compare the results of companies across the three ESG dimensions to provide both individual scores for each dimension and an overall score usually obtained by arithmetical mean. The main sustainability indexes are based on the ESG scores of companies and aim to identify those most attentive to the sustainable impact of their activities, in which it is convenient to invest (for example, Dow Jones Sustainability Index, FTSE4 Good, Stoxx Sustainability Index, or Euronext Vigeo Family (Liern & Pérez-Gladish, 2018).

Previous authors have already analyzed ESG rating agencies (Escrig-Olmedo et al., 2019), their strategies (Avetisyan & Hockerts, 2017), their evaluation processes and weighing systems (Chatterji et al., 2016; Escrig-Olmedo et al., 2010). Several authors have used these ESG ratings for their empirical research. However, few studies explore the origins, historical evolution, growth strategies of ESG rating agencies, and whether these ratings are accurate or not (Avetisyan & Hockerts, 2017; Chatterji et al., 2016).

While there is complete agreement on the importance of ESG investments, there is a clear divergence on what constitutes a sustainable investment (Delmas & Blass, 2010). ESG ratings provided by various ESG rating agencies significantly diverge (Chatterji et al., 2016; Billio et al., 2021; Berg et al., 2022), and homogeneity among the several ESG ratings is generally low (Christensen et al., 2022). The disparity in ratings dilutes the impact of ESG performance ratings on asset prices, making it unlikely that ESG performance will be reflected in share and corporate bond prices (De Santis et al., 2020).

Escrig-Olmedo et al., 2019 analyze the ESG rating agencies market from 2008 to 2018. The authors note that the ESG rating sector has grown significantly through the new entry of financial rating agencies and information providers and has undergone a phase of consolidation through merger and acquisition processes between existing ESG rating agencies. The different methodologies used by the rating agencies coincide in consideration of the three measurement aspects (environmental, social, and governance). During the 10 years of analysis, an evolution emerged in the criteria used by the rating agencies in the three areas of analysis. The results show a greater interest in environmental issues, the fight against climate change, and mitigating greenhouse gas emissions. As regards the criteria of the social sphere, after the definition of the Sustainable Development Goals (SDGs), some aspects have become essential for the rating agencies in order to measure the corporate contribution to sustainable development. In particular, factors related to improving health and education, reducing inequalities, and the need to stimulate economic growth. Finally, as regards the aspects of corporate governance, compared to the past, they seem to acquire greater importance in the evaluation, especially those concerning the prevention of corruption and extortion. The authors conclude their work by analyzing a sample of nine ESG rating agencies. The analysis shows that all the ESG rating agencies in the sample incorporate the dimensions of sustainability in their assessment process, but not always in a balanced way. The authors report the example of RobecoSAM, which does not consider the three dimensions of sustainability in a balanced way but gives each dimension a weight in the evaluation without clarifying how it was defined.

From this point of view, there is no lack of criticism on ESG ratings or on particular areas and on their ability to distinguish which companies are socially responsible (Avetisyan & Hockerts, 2017). With the possibility that such ratings produce uncertain and misleading results for stakeholders (Entine, 2003). In their study, Chatterji et al. (2016) give the example of companies with high ESG ratings despite being involved in more or less important scandals. These same companies get different ratings from various agencies. According to the authors, this lack of convergence is linked to the difficulty of measuring societies' contribution to sustainable development with certainty and reliability. This uncertainty and discrepancy in results should translate into caution on the part of users of ESG ratings. Drawing business conclusions based on these findings could be misleading. Investors who ignore these issues and base their strategies on the results of a single rating agency may end up investing in a portfolio of companies that are only "subjectively" sustainable (Rzeźnik et al., 2021).

Similarly, Semenova and Hassel (2015), analyzing the correspondence of the environmental ratings of four agencies, show that the ratings use the same domains but do not converge overall. Furthermore, several studies have demonstrated the heterogeneity of measurement approaches (Delmas & Blass, 2010); Hedesström et al., 2011). Therefore, the possibility that ESG data does not validly and reliably reflect the organizational reality, thus nullifying the contribution of sustainable investments to sustainable development (Busch et al., 2016).

## 3 The Main ESG Rating Agencies

Numerous rating agencies provide business performance indicators based on ESG criteria. Traditional rating agencies have begun to consider the ESG information necessary to assess company performance. This has made companies more attentive and aware of sustainability because the result achieved influences their image.

ESG rating agencies connect stakeholders and companies by providing stakeholders with essential information on the ESG performance of companies (Rahdari & Anvary Rostamy, 2015). Many of the ESG rating agencies were founded in the late 1990s (Avetisyan & Ferrary, 2013) in the process of acquisitions and mergers that led to many agencies changing their names, while others disappeared, often taken over by a competitor (Escrig-Olmedo et al., 2019). As Avetisyan and Hockerts (2017), there are 2 growth strategies followed by rating agencies over the years. The first strategy is based on organic growth and the creation of a network of alliances (for example, RobecoSAM). The second strategy is developed through mergers and acquisitions (for example, Vigeo Eiris) or through the entry into the ESG rating sector of previous data providers (for example, MSCI).

The three rating agencies that we analyze, also considering the acquisitions and mergers that have seen them as protagonists, have been among the main and most active international players in the ESG rating sector. Each of the agencies establishes its methodology for defining the ESG rating. Most of the procedures followed are quite similar, deviating, in some cases, in the indication of the final value expressed in different ways.

Morgan Stanley Capital International—MSCI ESG Research is a leading ESG rating agency that analyzes thousands of companies' environmental, social and governance practices worldwide. With over 1500 ESG equity and bond indexes, it joins the ESG rating industry lagging behind other agencies but has grown rapidly through a few acquisitions in recent years. MSCI is the result of the acquisition of several ESG research providers. In particular, in 2010, RiskMetrics acquired a provider of risk management and governance products and services, which had previously acquired ISS (Institutional Shareholder Services) in 2007 and Innovest and KLD in 2009. These acquisitions enabled MSCI to obtain the knowledge, skills, methods, and clients of the two industry-leading rating agencies in previous decades. Subsequently, in 2019, MSCI acquired Carbon Delta, establishing the MSCI Climate Risk Center in Zurich. These acquisitions have led MSCI to scale up its business by integrating big data delivery with ESG information (Fig. 3.1).

MSCI focuses on the intersection of a company's business and important ESG issues. It provides ESG information to institutional investors on significant risks and opportunities in order to distribute capital in a way that maximizes investment returns. In addition, MSCI ESG Research data and ratings are used to construct the MSCI ESG indexes. Their ESG ratings range from leading (AAA, AA), medium (A, BBB, BB) to laggard (B, CCC). (https://www.msci.com/).

Vigeo Eiris Moody's ESG Solutions Group was born after a series of acquisitions. Vigeo was founded in 2002 and acquired the French rating agency Arèse in

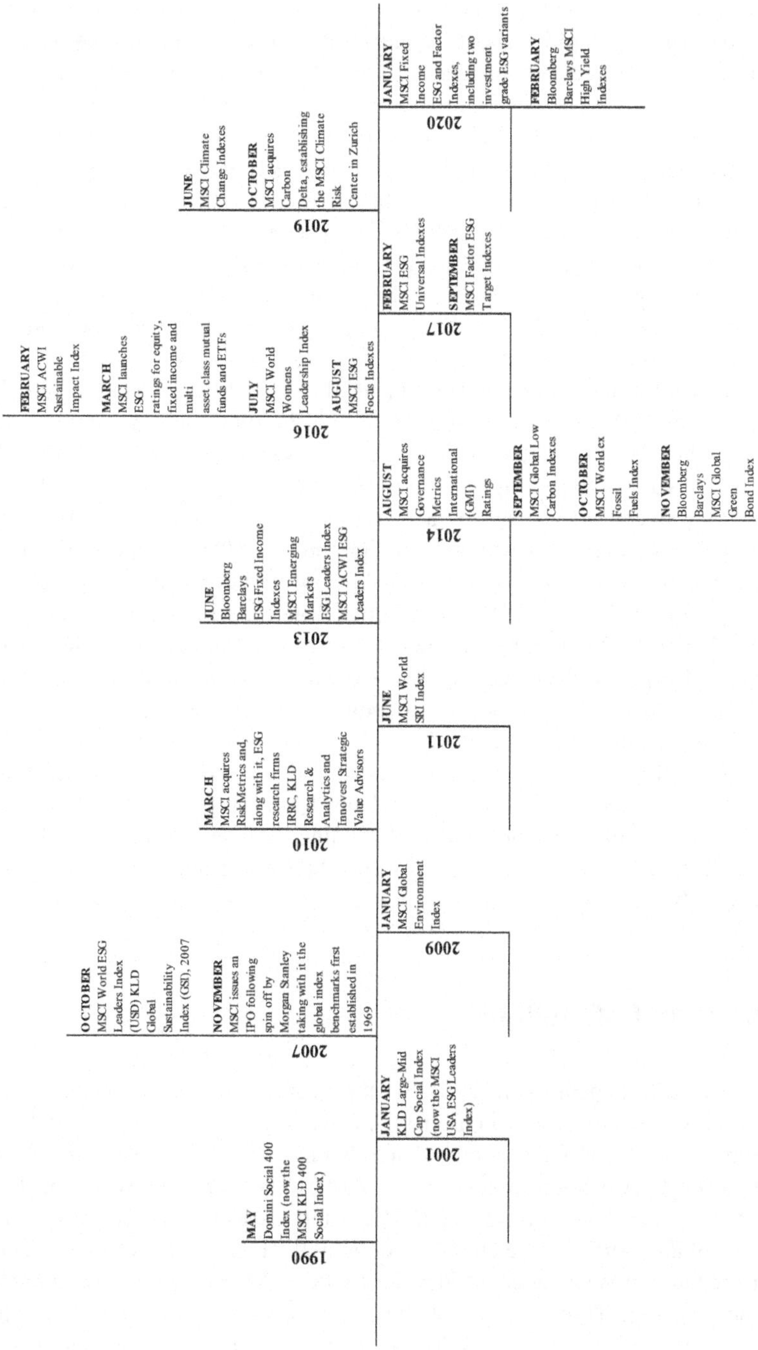


**Fig. 3.1** The growth of MSCI. Source: https://www.msci.com/

2003, quickly acquiring a leadership position. EIRIS, on the other hand, was founded in the UK in 1983 as a non-profit organization. Its initial activity was to inform churches and charities about the ethical dimensions of their investments. In 2015 the two rating agencies merged to create Vigeo Eiris. In 2019 Vigeo Eiris (VE) was acquired by Moody's Corporation and joined Moody's ESG Solutions Group in 2020. Therefore, the VE brand is replaced with Moody's ESG Solutions becoming a general reference point in the ESG field. VE provides an ESG rating for each company, which is given by the weighted average of the individual scores that measure the degree to which companies take into account and manage environmental, social and governance factors (Business Behavior (BB); Corporate Governance (CG); Community Involvement (CIN); Environment (ENV); Human Resources (HR); Human Rights (HRT)). Its ESG ratings take values between 0 and 100. (https://vigeo-eiris.com/).

S&P Global, formerly McGraw Hill Financial, Inc., until 2016 and McGraw Hill Companies until 2013 entered the financial sector in 1966 with the acquisition of Standard & Poor's. Substantial corporate growth saw S&P Global acquire ESG ratings and ESG benchmarking activities from RobecoSAM (SAM) in January 2020. SAM was created in 1995 by a Swiss investment banker and was the first ESG rating agency to partner with an index provider in 1999 when the DJSI (Dow Jones Sustainability Index) was launched. After some intermediate steps, Robeco completely acquired SAM in 2010 and renamed RobecoSAM in 2013 (Avetisyan & Hockerts, 2017). In 2020, the S&P Global acquisition from RobecoSAM (SAM) included the Corporate Sustainability Assessment (CSA) brand, an annual assessment of the sustainability practices of a company, regarded as "the leading ESG assessment for quality and usefulness by global sustainability professionals." Since 1999, SAM and S&P Dow Jones Index have collaborated to use the CSA as a performance indicator for inclusion in the Dow Jones Sustainability Index (DJSI) and the new family of S&P ESG indexes, including the S&P 500 ESG and the S&P Global 1200 ESG. Its ESG ratings take values between 0 and 100. (https://www.spglobal.com/).

## 4 The Main ESG Indexes

The Dow Jones Sustainability Index (DJSI), the most recognized sustainability index in the world, was the first index in its class, created jointly in 1999 by the S&P Dow Jones and RobecoSAM indexes and identifies the most sustainable companies in 61 sectors (de Castro Sobrosa Neto et al., 2020). The DJSI indexes, considering environmental, social and governance (ESG) criteria, select the companies with the best sustainability performance among those with the highest capitalization. This is done on the basis of the assessments developed through the Corporate Sustainability Assessment (CSA). Through a questionnaire, a score is assigned annual which includes elements of "corporate governance items, media and stakeholder analysis, risk and crisis management, codes of conduct/compliance/corruption and bribery, supply chain management, tax strategy, environmental and social reporting, operational eco-efficiency, labor practice indicators and human rights, human capital development, talent attraction and retention, corporate citizenship and philanthropy and a GRI mapping" (Landi & Sciarelli, 2019). The DJSI is based on a best-in-class approach, which includes companies from all sectors with superior performance in terms of sustainability. Based on the evaluation elements, a score is assigned, and companies from all sectors that rank in the top 10% are included in the DJSI World. The Dow Jones Sustainability Index family includes global, regional, and national benchmarks (DJSI World; DJSI North America; DJSI Europe; DJSI Asia Pacific; DJSI Emerging Markets; DJSI Korea; DJSI Australia; DJSI Chile; DJSI MILA Pacific Alliance). (https://www.spglobal.com/esg/performance/indices/djsi-index-family).

The Financial Times Stock Exchange for Good (FTSE4Good) was created in 2001 by the London Stock Exchange. The FTSE4Good indexes group the best companies for sustainability performance based on analyses conducted by FTSE Russel and measure the performance of companies that demonstrate sound environmental, social and governance (ESG) practices. A wide variety of market participants has used it since it is a benchmark for monitoring the performance of sustainable investment portfolios. These indexes are used worldwide because they allow for identifying sustainable companies, carrying out benchmarking analyses, and generally measuring company performance (de Castro Sobrosa Neto et al., 2020). The indexes are derived from the FTSE Global Equity Index Series. They certainly are a tool for SRIs because they show companies with a better impact in terms of sustainability. The same FTSE4Good criteria are also applied to the FTSE Developed and FTSE Emerging series of indexes, covering over 23 developed and 20 emerging countries (https://www.ftserussell.com/products/indices/ftse4good).

MSCI ESG are indexes that arise from the input provided by MSCI ESG ratings. The MSCI indexes have grown significantly over the years and today count over 1500 ESG equity and bond indexes. From this point of view, MSCI exploits its role as a leader in decision support tools on SRI. Global sustainability indexes include companies with higher ESG ratings than their industry competitors (Bielinskyi et al., 2020). Domini 400 Social Index (now MSCI KLD 400 Social Index) was the first index launched in 1990 and is considered the first sustainable and responsible investment (SRI) index. MSCI KLD 400 Social Index is designed to expose companies with high MSCI ESG ratings, while excluding companies whose products may have adverse social or environmental impacts. It consists of 400 selected US small-, medium-, and large-capitalization companies. (https://www.msci.com/our-solutions/indexes/esg-indexes).

STOXX Global ESG Leaders Index, a group of indexes characterized by a transparent structure based on ESG indicators provided by Sustainalytics. The indexes are managed by STOXX, the owner of some of the most important international equity indexes, such as the STOXX50 (Bielinskyi et al., 2020). Launched in 2011, these indexes select the best stocks by ESG performance among the 1800 present in the general STOXX Global index. The index consists of three ESG sub-indexes: STOXX Global ESG Environmental Leaders, STOXX Global ESG

Social Leaders, and STOXX Global ESG Governance Leaders. To be included in the Global ESG Leaders Index, it is necessary to be included in at least one of the three indexes. (https://www.stoxx.com/index-details?symbol=SXWESGP).

Euronext Vigeo Eiris are indexes developed by the rating agency Vigeo Eiris—Moody's ESG Solutions. These indexes include the companies that have achieved the best ratings, in terms of ESG performance, according to the evaluations of Vigeo Eiris—Moody's ESG Solutions. This range of indexes is updated periodically every six months. It includes Euronext VE World 120, Euronext V. E Europe 120, Euronext VE Eurozone 120, Euronext VE EM 70, Euronext VE US 50, Euronext VE France 20, Euronext VE United Kingdom 20, and Euronext VE Benelux 20. (https://vigeo-eiris.com/solutions-investors/esg-indices-ranking/indices-euronext-v-e/).

The United Nations Global Compact 100 ("GC 100") global index, developed by Sustainalytics, includes the 100 companies that have distinguished themselves globally on environmental, social and governance (ESG) issues and respect the ten fundamental principles of United Nations on human rights, labor, environment, and anti-corruption. (https://www.unglobalcompact.org/take-action/action/global-compact-100).

## 5 Non-financial Performance Reporting

Any type of policy adopted is perceived if and to the extent that the results can be measured and communicated. Communication contributes to the formation of corporate identity and reduces the distance between the real image of the company and that perceived by the outside world. To communicate the company's ethical and social commitment to take place clearly, a series of ethical, social, and environmental certifications have been created for company management. The literature often refers to the theme in a heterogeneous and constantly evolving way "company social accounts," "social accounting," "social and environmental relationship," and "social and environmental accounting" (Eugénio et al., 2010).

The increasing need to share and compare the results achieved, also intending to impact on sustainable development, has resulted in the need to improve management and communication tools (Tenuta, 2009). This has led to the creation of tools to aid in the definition and formalization of corporate management, for the verification of accountability processes, for reporting (social report, environmental report, sustainability report), up to the most common social support systems (investments in the community, donations, and sponsorships). The ethical certification makes the ethical dimension of the management system visible and more credible than in the past, creating an advantage for the company that can be traced back to the possibility of obtaining benefits in terms of comparison with its competitors.

Taking into account the overall value generated by one's business, illustrating the consistency between the declared values and objectives and the behaviors then implemented is an opportunity for the company to renew the trust that nourishes the relationship with its various interlocutors. Financial reporting does not provide a complete view of a firm's activities and impacts (Guthrie & Farneti, 2008). For this reason, organizations of all types combine traditional forms of financial statements and reporting with new documents that aim to present the performance of the company as a whole, also illustrating how the value produced was generated and what effects. Their business activities have spread over the company, the territory, and the environment.

Social and environmental disclosure (SED) can be considered an example of corporate social and environmental sustainability (Martin-Sardesai & Guthrie, 2020). Until the introduction of Directive 2014/95/EU, in Europe, the SED was voluntary (Delbard, 2008) and only later, for some companies, did it become mandatory.

It is difficult to establish the exact moment companies began to look at the social and environmental aspects. However, several authors trace this interest between 1960 and 1970 (Parker, 2005). Fifka (2012) highlights five periods in the development of SED research starting from the 1970s. Based on this report, we analyze, in the following paragraphs, the reporting documents starting from the classic models that separate financial information from non-financial information and then moving on to integrated models (Venturelli et al., 2017), which include both types of information in order to provide stakeholders with comprehensive summary data on company performance (Maas et al., 2016).

## 6 The Social and Environmental Balance

Social reporting is the earliest form of reporting on non-financial matters that can be traced back to the early 1970s (Fifka, 2012). At that time, environmental disclosure did not have its representation but was incorporated into social (Mathews, 1997). Concerns about disclosure of information to employees, collective bargaining, the role of trade unions, and broader theoretical questions about the nature of work and occupation were dominating (Eugénio et al., 2010).

The term "social," as an adjective for "balance sheet," indicates that the document contains information about the reporting of the social activity that the company carried out during the year (Hinna, 2002).

The expression social report indicates a document that certainly does not have the same technical characteristics as the financial statements but has several points in common with it, starting from the information function and the fact that they are both final documents that generally interest the stakeholders. Therefore, the social report is an ethical and social integration to the economic and financial representation of the financial statements (Tenuta, 2009).

The motivation that drives companies to draft the social report is of an informative and communication nature and arises from the need to inform stakeholders.

The social report is a reporting model on the quality and quantity of relations between an organization and its stakeholders to provide a homogeneous, complete, and transparent picture of the interdependence between economic and social factors deriving from an organization's choices (Rubino, 2007).

Through this tool, the social and ethical commitment of the company is communicated to the stakeholders. It explains the identity, the system of values assumed by the company, the methods of interaction with the environment and highlights how these are translated into selection criteria, management behaviors and results, while setting out the improvement objectives that the company is committed to pursuing, and is the added value and its distribution.

The Global Reporting Initiative defines it as a reporting model of the quantity and quality of the relationship between the company and the reference groups representative of the entire community, necessary to outline a homogeneous, punctual, complete and transparent framework on the complex interdependence between the economic and socio-political factors connected and consequent to the choices made.

The social report already boasts an established tradition: it accompanies the financial statements and represents, for the company combination, on the one hand, a vector of further and more targeted information and, on the other, a tool for acquiring social consensus. It detects the social impact of company decisions and therefore involves employment, working conditions, and safety issues.

In for-profit structures, the social report can be considered a communication tool with stakeholders to support the company in public opinion as a socially responsible structure, while, in non-profit structures, the social balance has a function of "social legitimation" that operates in the reference community and therefore aggregates economic resources—fundraising—human resources—volunteering (Puntillo, 2008).

Social responsibility must be part of the company's mission, which must behave consistently with this approach in all fields of its business. It is also desirable that the company builds its policy with the stakeholders, who can make an important contribution to companies in terms of identifying the strengths and weaknesses of the company's image.

Therefore, every company should clearly communicate its commitments and results in terms of social responsibility. The absence of communication creates distance with the stakeholders, who are deprived of knowledge of an important part of the business and, above all, precludes the spread of an ethical business culture (Rubino, 2007).

The social report is based on the principle that the interaction with stakeholders is not attributable only to economic relationships and cannot be measured only in terms of economic-financial magnitudes. Furthermore, there can be various needs that lead to the drafting of this tool:

1. means of external communication.
2. means to improve the organization, management, internal communication.
3. institutional means.
4. means to elaborate a social strategy.
5. means to identify one's social mission (Rusconi, 2006).

In particular, the social report should:

(a) allow an understanding of the role played by the organization in civil society.
(b) be a tool capable of providing information on the achievement of the social objectives set.
(c) highlight that the purpose of the company is not only to create profit but also to add value for the community.
(d) be a moment of reflection on the commitment that one has within the organization to improve product and service quality, relationship with consumers, safety in the workplace, respect for the environment, etc. (Di Giandomenico, 2008).

The experience of social balances seems to demonstrate the spread of a cultural change that begins to conceive the real dimension of a company which has as its main objective the creation of socio-economic value for the entire community (Fazzi, 2005).

The social report was a significant step that brought the organization closer to its stakeholders by creating an open and fruitful dialogue process based on the principles of accountability and clarity. The experience of the social report is undoubtedly positive, as it is an element capable of developing phases of change and important support for strategic-managerial, communication and stakeholder participation processes. In fact, through the social report, the organization can focus on what it has produced and represent it externally.

Since the 1990s, pollution issues have gained more weight and the first environmental reports were born. According to Mathews and Perera (1996) when the topic of the environment gained importance, it became almost an autonomous domain for which social and environmental information were analyzed together or separately. In several cases, the social and environmental areas were contained in a single document (Hahn & Kühnen, 2013), in which environmental reporting was often generally considered a subset of social reporting (Adams, 2004). In an analysis carried out by Parker (2005) on publications from 1988 to 2003, it emerges that 66% of publications concern the environmental sphere, 25% concern the social sphere exclusively, while 9% analyze both areas. Since the 1990s, the relationship between business and the environment has been changing towards the awareness that the environment cannot be considered only a container of resources to be used without economic quantification but is a real productive factor for the organization. Traditional control systems characterized by financial, equity, and economic analyses are inadequate for measuring, understanding, and controlling the environmental dimension of the company.

According to Eugénio et al., 2010, in the 1990s, companies assumed greater attention to disclosures regarding environmental issues than to social ones. For this reason, many companies have begun to deal more with the environment through reporting tools focused only on environmental issues (Adams, 2004).

The representation of the environmental dimension is possible through integrating traditional tools with an information tool aimed at verifying the environmental variable in the final balance. From this point of view, the environmental balance is configured as an instrument capable of representing the relationships between the company and the environment. The environmental balance takes its name from the equality of purpose it has concerning the traditional balance, understood in economic-financial terms. In fact, both tools refer to the results obtained by the organization, over some time, obviously on different management areas (Cisi, 2003). This has led companies to manage better their environmental impact (Wilmshurst & Frostr, 2000), and understand that this can affect corporate value (Eugénio et al., 2010).

The Environmental Balance is a voluntary "control" tool available to any organization, public or private, to develop a more in-depth knowledge of environmental issues related to its management activities.

Environmental accounting originates from the need to deepen the measurement of the effects of corporate decisions on the environment to the information inferred from traditional accounting tools. This type of accounting makes it possible to evaluate the environmental impact of economic policies and the costs of economic development paid in terms of pollution, costs for restoration and compensation.

The final objective of environmental accounting is the construction of the environmental balance intended as a conjunctive tool between the external environment and the organization, from which it is possible to infer physical data, relating both to the natural resources used as inputs in the production processes, on emissions into the atmosphere, on water discharges, on waste and noise produced by the activities carried out by the organization, and monetary data relating to the expenditure incurred by the organization for the protection of the environment (Puntillo, 2008).

The environmental balance is an information document that describes the main relationships between the organization and the environment in which the following indicators are contained:

- environmental management, which serves to evaluate the control activity carried out by the organization on environmental aspects.
- absolute environmental, which measures the impact factors created by the organization.
- environmental performance, which measures environmental efficiency.
- the potential effect, through which the effects that the business activity could produce on the environment are assessed.
- environment effect, which evaluates the effects that the business activity generates.

Through this communication tool, stakeholders are provided with all the information necessary to understand the actions taken, the resources used, and the results obtained by the organization in carrying out its business. The subjects most interested in this information are:

(a) customers and consumers, in order to verify the eco-compatibility characteristics of the products.
(b) workers, to learn about the risks associated with their business.
(c) environmental groups, with reference to the environmental impact of the choices of the organization.

(d) financial institutions and shareholders for monitoring the possible causes of environmental risks.
(e) local communities, with regard to the negative consequences of external diseconomies caused by production processes.
(f) governmental control bodies, in order to know the characteristics and effects of the environmental management systems adopted by the organizations.
(g) suppliers, business partners, etc. as regards possible causes of limitation in the reliability of the organization.
(h) trade associations regarding the collection of information on environmental protection on a sectoral basis.

The formation of the environmental balance is developed in three phases:

1. The first phase involves the collection of data that it is considered useful to observe, and at the same time, they are classified according to the pre-established purposes.
2. In the second phase, the data collected must be processed in order to transform the data collected into an environmental balance.
3. In the third phase, the processed data and information are communicated.

Through this external communication tool, stakeholders are provided with a series of items of environmental information in terms of:

(a) actions are taken for environmental protection.
(b) resources used.
(c) expected results (Cisi, 2003).

The dissemination of environmental performance, through the environmental report, was mainly aimed at reporting high performance in the initial stages (Schreck & Raithel, 2018). The role acquired by the environment in modern business management is necessarily linked to the awareness that the indiscriminate exploitation of natural resources can lead to a crisis of unsustainability. A company that does not take into account the burden it produces on the environment in its decision-making processes attributes the costs to the community according to an "outsourcing process." Therefore, it is important to underline that, even being a "voluntary" instrument, the benefits deriving from the preparation of the environmental balance are important both on the management level in order to monitor environmental performance not only as regards costs and waste (assessment of the level of protection and enhancement of the territory; assessment of the use of tools with a lower environmental impact; development of tools increasingly suitable for environmental communication, etc.), both in terms of image in the relationships with stakeholders. However, as often happens for documents of a voluntary nature, there is no univocal scheme or generally recognized methodologies that make the financial statements homogeneous and comparable, thus leaving ample room for discretion (Tenuta, 2009).

## 7 The Sustainability Report

Since the early 2000s, social reporting has, in fact, been integrated into sustainability reporting (Parker, 2005; Daub, 2007), which includes and integrates the three economic, social, and environmental areas (Hahn & Kühnen, 2013), providing more conclusive results (Qiu et al., 2016).

The sustainable organization seeks financial stability and, at the same time, acts under social expectations by minimizing its own negative environmental impacts (Jonas, 1978). Environmental, economic, and social problems are combined. On the other hand, the Lisbon Strategy, a reference point for the political commitment of the European Union for economic and social renewal, highlights sustainable development as the main element in order to examine the economic, social, and environmental effects in decision-making processes of the initiatives undertaken (triple bottom approach).

The necessary attention to sustainability has led all organizations to determine their own sustainable performance by identifying and communicating the economic, environmental, and social impacts produced. The document which illustrates the efforts made by the organization to reference the impacts that its actions have on the economic, social, and environmental sphere of reference is called the sustainability report. In the 2001 Green Paper, the sustainability report is defined as: "The voluntary integration of companies' social and ecological concerns in their commercial operations and in their relations with interested parties." Creating a summary document on the economic, environmental, and social impacts is an increasingly recurring custom, the result of both the pressure of the interest groups and the advantages that the company achieves in terms of image and credibility. In the literature, the most important benefit found is the improvement of reputation and corporate image (Friedman & Miles, 2001; Armitage & Marston, 2008; Unerman, 2008) in addition to improving transparency, brand value, and employee motivation to support the company's internal control processes (Brooks & Oikonomou, 2018). According to Castilla-Polo and Sánchez-hernández (2020), the SED would be an essential element and a predictor of corporate reputation.

In addition, national and international governmental institutions under pressure from interest groups have been and are very active in forcefully asking companies to account for their objectives and the consequences of their behavior in terms of quality of life, environmental protection, and respect for a man (Paris, 2003). While the social and environmental reports highlight the impacts of company management on the social aspects and the ecosystem, respectively, the sustainability report is a synthesis in economic, social, and environmental terms. It makes it possible to include, in a single document, multiple aspects deriving from corporate action, namely financial, economic, social, and environmental ones. For this reason, we speak of triple bottom line reporting (Romolini, 2006).

The sectoral approach obtained from the environmental and social balance sheets does not allow for a transversal comparison that connects the social effects of environmental policies and the environmental effects of social policies, which instead occurs in the construction of the sustainability report (Vaccari, 2005).

The sustainability report is a reporting, planning and strategic control tool that allows one to evaluate an organization according to the logic of economic efficiency, environmental protection, and social protection. The usefulness of this type of tool is linked to:

1. the improvement of governance processes allowing the management of the conflict between the three social, economic, and environmental variables.
2. the improvement of the integration processes of sectoral policies.
3. the analysis of the elements of conflict between environmental, social, and economic policies and the description of the equilibrium point reached.
4. greater transparency in reporting and greater involvement of stakeholders and internal staff.

The Global Reporting Initiative (GRI) takes on great importance in terms of sustainability. GRI was founded in 1997 by the Coalition for Environmentally Responsible Economies and the United Nations Environment Program founded in Boston by environmental associations, institutional investors, socially responsible investors, and religious organizations in partnership with the United Nations Environment Program (UNEP), whose mission is to create a credible and reliable system for sustainability reporting. Indeed, through sustainability reporting, it is possible to provide a balanced and reasonable representation of an organization's sustainability performance, including the negative and positive impacts generated by management operations (Rubino et al., 2016).

The first version of the GRI Guidelines (G1) was published in 2000 and provided the first global framework for sustainability reporting. In 2002, the first update of the guidelines (G2) was launched and then expanded and improved in 2006, 2011, and 2013 with the G3, G3.1, and G4.

This report applied to any type of organization and, therefore, to the public sector. Furthermore, to better represent the Public Administration sector, a specific supplement was developed called Sector supplement for public agencies. In this type of model, in addition to the three standard sections modified and integrated to adapt to the needs of local authorities, regions, and the state, a further one called "public policies and measurement systems" was added, in which public policies, the degree of importance and the methods of measurement were illustrated. The guidelines for sustainability reporting contained the Reporting Principles, the Reporting Guide, and the Standard Disclosure. The first part presented the Principles and the Reporting Guide for:

- the definition of the report content,
- guarantee the quality of information,
- the definition of the reporting perimeter.

Through this first part, the report's content was defined to guarantee the quality of the information and the reporting perimeter.

Once the contents and scope of the Report had been established, in the second part of the GRI guidelines, a subdivision into three parts of the structure of the sustainability report was identified:

1. The strategy and profile highlighted the general context that allowed the performance of the organization to be deciphered. Within this macro-area, there were four sections:

   (a) The first strategy and analysis section provided insights into strategic topics through a declaration on the importance of sustainability for the organization, the strategic priorities, the main events that had characterized the reporting period, the judgments on performance with respect to the objectives set, the perspectives on future objectives and any other aspects that referred to the strategic approach of the organization.
   (b) In the second section, the organization was described from the point of view of structure, size, and production.
   (c) The third section defined the report parameters or a series of general information on the reporting period of the information provided, the date of publication, the reporting periodicity, the objectives and scope of the report, which also contained an explanatory table of the contents of the report (GRI content index).
   (d) In the fourth section on governance, commitments, and stakeholder engagement, a series of information on the governance structure of the organization, on the commitment to external initiatives, and on the involvement of stakeholders was aggregated, largely contained in the report.

2. The management methods of the organization with reference to the stable aspects for each category of the information.
3. The performance indicators represented the three categories: environmental, social, and economic. Generic core indicators were distinguished and consequently presumably usable by most organizations regardless of their nature and additional indicators which by their nature could be relevant only for some organizations. The economic performance indicators referred not only to the financial results but also to the presence on the market and to the indirect economic impacts, while the environmental performance indicators were divided into different aspects: that of raw materials, energy, water, biodiversity, emissions, discharges and waste, products and services, compliance, transport and a general aspect of expenditure and investments for environmental protection. On the other hand, with reference to social performance, the relevant aspects referred to work practices, human rights, society and product responsibility.

Ultimately, each organization that applied the GRI model had, based on its own assessment of the content of the report and applying the "GRI application levels," declared the level of application of its report. There were three levels of application of the Global Reporting Initiative and reflected the degree of use of the guidelines issued by the GRI (A, B, C). To these three levels it was possible to add a plus (+) by self-declaring one's reporting level (Tenuta, 2009; Rija & Tenuta, 2010).

In 2016, GRI identified guidelines to define the first global standards for sustainability reporting. The *GRI Standards* constitute a reporting framework for all organizations and *are the most used globally to communicate their impacts through sustainability reporting*. The revised standards in 2021 is the most significant update since the GRI focused on setting standards. The GRI standards consist of a modular and interdependent structure to best create economic, social, and environmental reports. Reporting in compliance with the GRI Standards makes it possible to highlight the impacts on the economy, the environment, human rights and more generally on people. This allows for evaluations and informed decisions about the contribution of the organization to sustainable development. With the addition of the Sector Standards, the GRI Standards now comprise three series:

- Universal Standards revised in 2021 to enter into force on 01 January 2023; they incorporate the human rights and environmental due diligence reporting. The Universal Standards contain the reporting requirements and principles that all organizations must comply with to report in accordance with the GRI Standards. "The Universal Standards now reflect expectations for responsible business conduct in authoritative intergovernmental instruments such as the United Nations (UN) Guiding Principles on Business and Human Rights, the Organization for Economic Co-operation and Development (OECD) Guidelines for Multinational Enterprises, the OECD Due Diligence Guidance for Responsible Business Conduct, the International Labor Standards, and the International Corporate Governance Network (ICGN) Global Governance Principles." They apply to all organizations and consist of GRI 1: Foundation 2021, GRI 2: General Disclosures 2021, GRI 3: Material Topics 2021.

  GRI 1 introduces the scope and system of the GRI Standards and clarifies the key concepts for sustainability reporting. It also specifies the reporting requirements and principles that the organization must comply with in order to report in accordance with the GRI Standards.

  GRI 2 contains information that the organization uses to illustrate its reporting practices and other organizational details related to governance. This information allows the profile of the organization and its impacts to be highlighted.

  GRI 3 provides guidance on determining materials topics, their determination process, and how to manage each topic.
- The new Sector Standards allow for more consistent reporting of specific impacts for 40 sectors, increasing organizations' quality, completeness, and consistency. Each Sector Standards consists of an initial section that provides an overview of the characteristics of the sector and the most relevant impacts on the economy, the environment, and people.
- Topic Standards adapted for use with revised Universal Standards list information relevant to a particular topic. The 2021 update did not change the content so the numbering and release year remain unchanged. Each standard contains an overview and detailed information on the topic and the ways in which organizations manage their impacts. After the withdrawal of three standards, because they have been incorporated into the revised Universal Standards, there are currently 31 Topic Standards. (https://www.globalreporting.org/) (Fig. 3.2).

The organization intending to report in accordance with the GRI Standards must meet all nine requirements (Fig. 3.3).

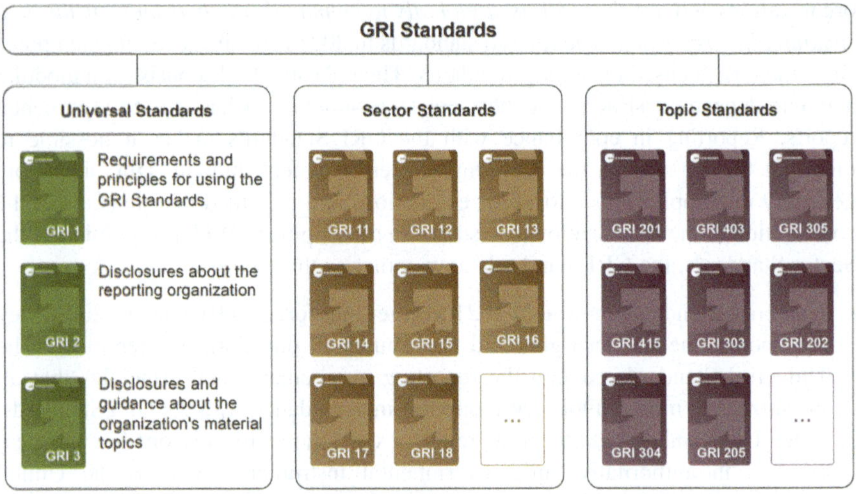


**Fig. 3.2** The GRI standards. Source: https://www.globalreporting.org/

| | |
|---|---|
| Requirement 1: | Apply the reporting principles |
| Requirement 2: | Report the disclosures in GRI 2: General Disclosures 2021 |
| Requirement 3: | Determine material topics |
| Requirement 4: | Report the disclosures in GRI 3: Material Topics 2021 |
| Requirement 5: | Report disclosures from the GRI Topic Standards for each material topic |
| Requirement 6: | Provide reasons for omission for disclosures and requirements that the organization cannot comply with |
| Requirement 7: | Publish a GRI content index |
| Requirement 8: | Provide a statement of use |
| Requirement 9: | Notify GRI |

**Fig. 3.3** Overview of in accordance requirements. Source: https://www.globalreporting.org/

Publish a GRI content index
Provide a statement of use
Notify GRI

**Fig. 3.4** Overview of requirements for reporting with reference to the GRI standards. Source: https://www.globalreporting.org/

The organization that does not meet each of the nine requirements does not produce a document "in accordance" with the GRI Standards. In this case, the organization can claim that it has prepared the report "with the reference" if it meets certain requirements (Fig. 3.4).

# 8 The Integrated Report

The last of the five stages of SED research development (Fifka, 2012) starts from 2010 and can be extended to the present day (Martin-Sardesai & Guthrie, 2020). Non-financial reporting experiences a moment of significant development (Ioannou & Serafeim, 2015; Luo et al., 2015; Wang et al., 2016) compared to the past with the emergence of Integrated Reporting (IR) which integrates the financial and non-financial information of companies.

The integrated report (IR) is a reporting tool that links financial and non-financial information in order to overcome the limits of traditional reporting and provide stakeholders with concise, complete and comparable information on the company's ability to create value (Veltri & Silvestri, 2015; Vitolla, Raimo, & Rubino, 2019a; Vitolla, Raimo, Rubino, & Garzoni, 2019b). The main objective of an integrated report is to demonstrate how an organization is able to create, preserve, or erode value over time by combining business inputs, activities, and outputs (Veltri & Silvestri, 2020). IR, therefore, means a new approach to corporate reporting that looks at the management of the company as a whole (Beattie & Smith, 2013; Farneti & Rammal, 2013) as well as a way to develop integrated thinking.

According to Veltri & Silvestri, 2020 on the annual report, IR focuses on creating value over time, rather than profits and losses, and on disclosure of information rather than measurement.

The International Integrated Reporting Council (IIRC) is a global coalition made up of regulators, investors, companies, regulators of financial accounting standards, professionals, academia, and nongovernmental organizations. Since 2010, its goal has been to develop and promote the use of integrated reporting (Kılıç & Kuzey, 2018). In 2011, the International Integrated Reporting Council (IIRC) published a document specifying that an IR should include material information on the strategy of an organization, governance, performance and prospects as well as reflect the business, social, and environmental context in which it operates (International Integrated Reporting Council (IIRC), 2011). In December 2013, the IIRC published its <IR> International Framework, replaced by an updated version in January 2021, to indicate the guiding principles and content elements that an IR must have as well as illustrate the fundamental concepts. The IR report must include quantitative and qualitative information while promoting integrated thinking (Atkins & Maroun, 2015).

The seven Guiding Principles that provide the content of the report and how the information is presented are applied both individually and as a whole (Fig. 3.5).

The eight content elements are questions to be answered because they are determined by the characteristics of the organization and are linked to each other and are not mutually exclusive (Fig. 3.6).

These principles and elements refer to the company's six capitals to create value (financial capital, productive capital, intellectual capital, human capital, social and relational capital, and natural capital). Not all capital is equally important or applicable in all organizations. The <IR> Framework focuses on changes in the value of

| | | |
|---|---|---|
| **Seven Guiding Principles underpin the preparation and presentation of an integrated report, informing the content of the report and how information is presented:** | ***Strategic focus and future orientation***. An integrated report should provide insight into the organization's strategy, and how it relates to the organization's ability to create value in the short, medium and long term, and to its use of and effects on the capitals | ***Materiality***. An integrated report should disclose information about matters that substantively affect the organization's ability to create value over the short, medium and long term |
| | ***Connectivity of information***. An integrated report should show a holistic picture of the combination, interrelatedness and dependencies between the factors that affect the organization's ability to create value over time | ***Conciseness***. An integrated report should be concise |
| | ***Stakeholder relationships***. An integrated report should provide insight into the nature and quality of the organization's relationships with its key stakeholders, including how and to what extent the organization understands, takes into account and responds to their legitimate needs and interests | ***Reliability and completeness***. An integrated report should include all material matters, both positive and negative, in a balanced way and without material error<br><br>***Consistency and comparability***. The information in an integrated report should be presented: (a) on a basis that is consistent over time; and (b) in a way that enables comparison with other organizations to the extent it is material to the organization's own ability to create value over time. |

**Fig. 3.5** Guiding principles. Source: https://www.integratedreporting.org/resource/international-ir-framework/

| | | |
|---|---|---|
| **An integrated report includes eight Content Elements that are fundamentally linked to each other and are not mutually exclusive:** | ***Organizational overview and external environment***. What does the organization do and what are the circumstances under which it operates? | ***Performance***. To what extent has the organization achieved its strategic objectives for the period and what are its outcomes in terms of effects on the capitals? |
| | ***Governance***. How does the organization's governance structure support its ability to create value in the short, medium and long term? | ***Outlook***. What challenges and uncertainties is the organization likely to encounter in pursuing its strategy, and what are the potential implications for its business model and future performance? |
| | ***Business model***. What is the organization's business model? | ***Basis of presentation***. How does the organization determine what matters to include in the integrated report and how are such matters quantified or evaluated? |
| | ***Risks and opportunities***. What are the specific risks and opportunities that affect the organization's ability to create value over the short, medium and long term, and how is the organization dealing with them? | |
| | ***Strategy and resource allocation***. Where does the organization want to go and how does it intend to get there? | |

**Fig. 3.6** Content elements. Source: https://www.integratedreporting.org/resource/international-ir-framework/

the capital of an enterprise that provides the value created. Organizations interact, in most cases, with all types of capital. However, in some cases, these interactions can be considered irrelevant for their inclusion in the integrated report (IIRC Framework, 2021).

Based on the <IR> International Framework, some private companies have begun to prepare and publish IR but in numbers that are still not significant (Pistoni et al., 2018; Landau et al., 2020) even if growing. Also, the debate in the literature has suffered from the reduced application focusing mainly on conceptual issues (Vitolla, Raimo, & Rubino, 2019a) and leaving out, instead, the empirical part on the consequences of IR (Maniora, 2017). Numerous studies agree on the lack of evidence in the literature of the benefits that are usually attributed to the IR Framework (de Graaff et al., 2019).

In this context, the EU 95/2014 Non-Financial Reporting Directive, analyzed in the next paragraph, plays an important role in promoting integrated reporting (Wahl et al., 2020) in order to increase the disclosure of environmental, social and governance (ESG) information of European organizations (La Torre et al., 2018).

## 9 Directive 2014/95/EU and Proposal for the Directive CSRD 2021/0104

The European legislation on "disclosure of non-financial and diversity information—the Non-financial Reporting Directive (NFRD)" was provided for by Directive 2014/95/EU (Lombardi, 2021). This directive establishes that starting from 2017, large companies in the Member States are required to provide a series of social, environmental, and governance declarations (Venturelli et al., 2017).

The disclosure of non-financial information (NFI) makes the disclosure of non-financial information *mandatory for large companies (with more than 500 employees), leaving it voluntary for SMEs*. The issue assumes even greater importance for listed companies for which the quality of the NFI is positively correlated with the company's share value (Wang et al., 2016).

The NFI can be based on existing standards and makes it possible to measure, monitor, and manage the results of companies and their impact on society. In practice, communicate to stakeholders the sustainability practices implemented by the company in the reference period (Kolk, 2005).

Pursuant to Directive 2014/95/EU, the non-financial information (NFI) that companies must provide has a minimum content that facilitates uniformity and comparability. Environmental, social, personnel, and compliance information of human rights are required in the fight against corruption. This information must be accurate to highlight the company's performance, its results, and the impact of its business. In particular, it is necessary to report:

- a brief description of the business model and the policies applied by the company,
- the result of these policies,

– the main risks associated with these aspects related to the activities of the company,
– the important non-financial key performance indicators for the specific activity of the company.

According to Venturelli et al. (2017), in the literature, there are criticisms of the NFI deriving from the lack of trust of stakeholders with respect to the information disclosed. Furthermore, the authors note that the European debate has highlighted the limitations of the directive, which, referring only to large companies, reduces its application and, therefore, its usefulness. In December 2019, owing to these reasons and, more generally, the lack of comparability, reliability and relevance of the non-financial information provided, the European Commission in its communication on the European Green Deal announced its intention to review the Non-financial Reporting Directive in order to consolidate the foundations for sustainable investments.

On April 21, 2021, the Commission presented its proposal for the Corporate Sustainability Reporting Directive (CSRD) 2021/0104, with the ultimate goal of bringing sustainability reporting to the same level as financial reporting by strengthening existing regulations. The proposal extends the scope to all large companies and all companies listed on regulated markets. This would lead to around 50,000 EU companies following the detailed sustainability reporting rules, up from 11,000 today. By identifying separate rules for SMEs, the Commission's proposal aims to facilitate the flow of information on corporate sustainability through the financial system. Therefore, companies are called upon to provide reliable and comparable information that is indispensable to investors and other stakeholders. The proposal to revise the current directive also focuses on simplifying reporting, allowing companies to use different sustainability reporting standards and frameworks. The novelties proposed in reporting are based on providing the company with a unique "one-stop-shop" solution. Furthermore, for greater clarity, the European Commission focuses on Taxonomy, with which it wants to overcome the confusion of reporting systems and classify economic activities that can be defined as sustainable.

## 10 The Sustainability Disclosure Standards (ISSB Standards)

The revision of the general rules and corporate reporting standards is addressed not only by the European Commission, which proposed the draft directive on sustainability but also by the IFRS Foundation (Tettamanzi et al., 2022).

In November 2021, the IFRS Foundation announced the creation of the International Sustainability Standards Board (ISSB). The ISSB aims to develop standards for companies to communicate their performance to investors (Eccles & Mirchandani, 2022). The formation of the ISSB is an initiative to consolidate sustainability reporting and disclosure frameworks from CDP, Climate Disclosure

Standard Board (CDSB), the Global Reporting Initiative (GRI), and Value Reporting Foundation (VRF). The ISSB will create one common comprehensive corporate reporting framework (Ditlev-Simonsen, 2022). The goal is to obtain transparent, reliable and comparable reporting on climate and other environmental, social and governance (ESG) issues.

On March 31, 2022, the ISSB published the draft exposures of the first two IFRS Sustainability Disclosure Standards (ISSB Standards) for public consultation (Exposure Draft IFRS S1 General Requirements for Disclosure of Sustainability-related Financial Information and Exposure Draft IFRS S2 Climate-related Disclosures). The drafts follow the prototype standards issued in 2021 and are released when the general interest within corporate information relating to sustainability is increasing.

The ISSB has indicated that its goal is that the complete set of ISSB standards, once finalized, provide a comprehensive global baseline of sustainability information for investors to assess companies' value.

Both at the international level, as regards the activities of the IASB and the IFRS Foundation, and at the European level, through the European Financial Reporting Advisory Group (EFRAG), corporate reporting is increasingly oriented towards the value that goes beyond financial results and the creation of value for shareholders only. What clearly emerges is the institutions' will to finally manage ESG dynamics from an accounting and reporting point of view (UK HM Treasury, 2021).

## References


Adams, C. A. (2004). The ethical, social and environmental reporting-performance portrayal gap. *Accounting, Auditing & Accountability Journal, 17*(5), 731–757. https://doi.org/10.1108/09513570410567791

Armitage, S., & Marston, C. (2008). Corporate disclosure, cost of capital and reputation: Evidence from finance directors. *British Accounting Review, 40*(4), 314–336. https://doi.org/10.1016/j.bar.2008.06.003

Atkins, J., & Maroun, W. (2015). Integrated reporting in South Africa in 2012: Perspectives from south African institutional investors. *Meditari Accountancy Research, 23*(2), 197–221. https://doi.org/10.1108/MEDAR-07-2014-0047

Avetisyan, E., & Ferrary, M. (2013). Dynamics of stakeholders' implications in the institutionalization of the CSR field in France and in the United States. *Journal of Business Ethics, 115*(1), 115–133. https://doi.org/10.1007/s10551-012-1386-3

Avetisyan, E., & Hockerts, K. (2017). The consolidation of the ESG rating industry as an enactment of institutional retrogression. *Business Strategy and the Environment, 26*(3), 316–330. https://doi.org/10.1002/bse.1919

Beattie, V., & Smith, S. J. (2013). Value creation and business models: Refocusing the intellectual capital debate. *British Accounting Review, 45*(4), 243–254. https://doi.org/10.1016/j.bar.2013.06.001

Bell, S., & Morse, S. (2008). *Sustainability indicators: Measuring the immeasurable?* (2nd ed.). Routledge. https://doi.org/10.4324/9781849772723

Berg, F., Koelbel, J.F., & Rigobon R. (2022), *Aggregate confusion: The divergence of ESG ratings, MIT Sloan school of management*, Working Paper.

Bielinskyi, A., Semerikov, S., Serdyuk, O., Solovieva, V., Soloviev, V., & Pichl, L. (2020). Econophysics of sustainability indices. *CEUR Workshop Proceedings, 2713*, 372–392.

Billio, M., Costola, M., Hristova, I., Latino, C., & Pelizzon, L. (2021). Inside the ESG ratings: (dis)agreement and performance. *Corporate Social Responsibility and Environmental Management, 28*(5), 1426–1445.

Boggia, A. (2007). Un modello di monitoraggio ambientale e socio-economico per la valutazione della sostenibilità. *Rivista Micron, 7.*

Brooks, C., & Oikonomou, I. (2018). The effects of environmental, social and governance disclosures and performance on firm value: A review of the literature in accounting and finance. *British Accounting Review, 50*(1), 1–15. https://doi.org/10.1016/j.bar.2017.11.005

Busch, T., Bauer, R., & Orlitzky, M. (2016). Sustainable development and financial markets: Old paths and new avenues. *Business and Society, 55*(3), 303–329. https://doi.org/10.1177/0007650315570701

Castilla-polo, F., & Sánchez-hernández, M. I. (2020). Testing social and environmental disclosure-reputation relationship: A longitudinal two-way analysis. *Sustainability Accounting, Management and Policy Journal, 12*(3), 548–570. https://doi.org/10.1108/SAMPJ-11-2019-0409

Cetindamar, D. (2007). Corporate social responsibility practices and environmentally responsible behavior: The case of the United Nations global compact. *Journal of Business Ethics, 76*, 163–176. https://doi.org/10.1007/s10551-006-9265-4

Chatterji, A. K., Durand, R., Levine, D. I., & Touboul, S. (2016). Do ratings of firms converge? Implications for managers, investors and strategy researchers. *Strategic Management Journal, 37*, 1597–1614. https://doi.org/10.1002/smj.2407

Chatterji, A. K., Levine, D. I., & Toffel, M. W. (2009). How well do social ratings actually measure corporate social responsibility? *Journal of Economics and Management Strategy, 18*(1), 125–169. https://doi.org/10.1111/j.1530-9134.2009.00210.x

Christensen, D. M., Serafeim, G., & Sikochi, A. (2022). Why is corporate virtue in the eye of the beholder? The case of ESG ratings. *The Accounting Review, 97*(1), 147–175.

Cisi, M. (2003). Il bilancio ambientale. *Giappichelli.*

Daub, C. H. (2007). Assessing the quality of sustainability reporting: An alternative methodological approach. *Journal of Cleaner Production, 15*(1), 75–85. https://doi.org/10.1016/j.jclepro.2005.08.013

de Castro Sobrosa Neto, R., de Lima, C. R. M., Bazil, D. G., de Oliveira Veras, M., & de Andrade Guerra, J. B. S. O. (2020). Sustainable development and corporate financial performance: A study based on the Brazilian corporate sustainability index (ISE). *Sustainable Development, 28*(4), 960–977. https://doi.org/10.1002/sd.2049

de Graaff, B., Steens, H. B. A., & Camfferman, K. (2019). Integrated reporting: Much ado about nothing? Available at *SSRN: https://ssrn.com/abstract=3382322*

De Santis, A., Di Marzo, G., Fasano, D., & Marlino, M. (2020). *Pricing risk adjusted: Il ruolo dei parametri ESG*, 1–47.

Delbard, O. (2008). CSR legislation in France and the European regulatory paradox: An analysis of EU CSR policy and sustainability reporting practice. *Corporate Governance, 8*(4), 397–405. https://doi.org/10.1108/14720700810899149

Delmas, M., & Blass, V. D. (2010). Measuring corporate environmental performance: The trade-offs of sustainability ratings. *Business Strategy and the Environment, 19*(4), 245–260. https://doi.org/10.1002/bse.676

Di Giandomenico, M. E. (2008). Il bilancio sociale e il modulo aziendale etico. *Giuffrè.*

Diez-Cañamero, B., Bishara, T., Otegi-Olaso, J. R., Minguez, R., & Fernández, J. M. (2020). Measurement of corporate social responsibility: A review of corporate sustainability indexes, rankings and ratings. *Sustainability, 12*(5). https://doi.org/10.3390/su12052153

Ditlev-Simonsen, C. D. (2022). Key tools for social- and environmental performance, and the UN sustainable development goals (SDGs). In *A guide to sustainable corporate responsibility*. Palgrave Macmillan. https://doi.org/10.1007/978-3-030-88203-7_4

Eccles, R. G., & Mirchandani, B. (2022). *We need universal ESG standards*. Retrieved from https://hbr.org/2022/02/we-need-universal-esg-accounting-standards

Entine, J. (2003). The myth of social investing: A critique of its practice and consequences for corporate social performance research. *Organization & Environment, 16*(3), 352–368. https://doi.org/10.1177/1086026603256283

Escrig-Olmedo, E., Fernández-Izquierdo, M., Ferrero-Ferrero, I., Rivera-Lirio, J. M., & Muñoz-Torres, M. J. (2019). Rating the raters: Evaluating how ESG rating agencies integrate sustainability principles. *Sustainability, 11*(3). https://doi.org/10.3390/su11030915

Escrig-Olmedo, E., Muñoz-Torres, M. J., & Fernandez-Izquierdo, M. A. (2010). Socially responsible investing: Sustainability indices, ESG rating and information provider agencies. *International Journal Sustainable Economy, 2*, 442–461.

Eugénio, T., Costa Lourenço, I., & Morais, A. I. (2010). Recent developments in social and environmental accounting research. *Social Responsibility Journal, 6*(2), 286–305. https://doi.org/10.1108/17471111011051775

Farneti, F., & Rammal, H. G. (2013, July 26–28). Sustainability reporting in the Italian public sector. Seventh Asia Pacific Interdisciplinary Research in Accounting Conference.

Fazzi, L. (2005). Questioni di fiducia: a cosa serve (e a cosa non serve) il bilancio sociale per le organizzazioni. *FrancoAngeli.*

Fifka, M. (2012). The development and state of research on social and environmental reporting in global comparison. *Journal fur Betriebswirtschaft, 62*(1). https://doi.org/10.1007/s11301-012-0083-8

Friedman, A. L., & Miles, S. (2001). Socially responsible investment and corporate social and environmental reporting in the UK: An exploratory study. *British Accounting Review, 33*(4), 523–548. https://doi.org/10.1006/bare.2001.0172

Gallopín, G. C. (1996). Environmental and sustainability indicators and the concept of situational indicators. A systems approach. *Environmental Modeling & Assessment, 1*(3), 101–117. https://doi.org/10.1007/bf01874899

Gardini, A., Cavaliere, G., Costa, M., Fanelli, L., & Parnolo P. (2003). Econometria. *FrancoAngeli.*

Guthrie, J., & Farneti, F. (2008). GRI sustainability reporting by Australian public sector organizations. *Public Money & Management, 28*(6), 361–366. https://doi.org/10.1111/j.1467-9302.2008.00670.x

Hahn, R., & Kühnen, M. (2013). Determinants of sustainability reporting: A review of results, trends, theory, and opportunities in an expanding field of research. *Journal of Cleaner Production, 59*, 5–21. https://doi.org/10.1016/j.jclepro.2013.07.005

Hedesström, M., Lundqvist, U., & Biel, A. (2011). Investigating consistency of judgement across sustainability analyst organizations. *Sustainable Development, 19*(2), 119–134. https://doi.org/10.1002/sd.511

Hinna, L. (2002). Il bilancio sociale: scenari, settori e valenze, modelli di rendicontazione sociale, gestione responsabile e sviluppo sostenibile, esperienze europee e casi italiani. *Il Sole 24 ore.*

Hockerts, K., & Moir, L. (2004). Communicating corporate responsibility to investors: The changing role of the investor relations function. *Journal of Business Ethics, 52*, 85–98.

Hutton, R. B., D'Antonio, L., & Johnsen, T. (1998). Socially responsible investing: Growing issues and new opportunities. *Business & Society., 37*(3), 281–305. https://doi.org/10.1177/000765039803700303

International Integrated Reporting Council (IIRC). (2021). *International IR framework.* Available at: https://www.integratedreporting.org/resource/international-ir-framework/

Ioannou, I., & Serafeim, G. (2015). The impact of corporate social responsibility on investment recommendations: Analysts' perceptions and shifting institutional logics. *Strategic Management Journal, 36*(7), 1053–1081. https://doi.org/10.1002/smj.2268

Jollands, N. (2006). Getting the most out of eco-efficiency indicators for policy. In P. A. Lawn (Ed.), *Sustainable development indicators in ecological economics* (pp. 317–343). Edward Elgar Publishing. https://doi.org/10.1504/IJARGE.2006.008163

Jonas, H. (1978). *Principio responsabilità*. Einaudi.

Kılıç, M., & Kuzey, C. (2018). Assessing current company reports according to the IIRC integrated reporting framework. *Meditari Accountancy Research, 26*(2), 305–333. https://doi.org/10.1108/MEDAR-04-2017-0138

Kolk, A. A. (2005). Decade of sustainability reporting: Developments and significance. *International Journal Environment and Sustainable Development, 3*, 51–64.

Kumar, S., Kumar, N., & Vivekadhish, S. (2016). Millennium development goals (MDGs) to sustainable development goals (SDGs): Addressing unfinished agenda and strengthening sustainable development and partnership. *Indian Journal Community Medicine, 41*, 1–11.

La Torre, M., Valentinetti, D., Dumay, J., & Rea, M. A. (2018). Improving corporate disclosure through XBRL: An evidence-based taxonomy structure for integrated reporting. *Journal of Intellectual Capital, 19*(2), 338–366. https://doi.org/10.1108/JIC-03-2016-0030

Landau, A., Rochell, J., Klein, C., & Zwergel, B. (2020). Integrated reporting of environmental, social, and governance and financial data: Does the market value integrated reports? *Business Strategy and the Environment, 29*(4), 1750–1763. https://doi.org/10.1002/bse.2467

Landi, G., & Sciarelli, M. (2019). Towards a more ethical market: The impact of ESG rating on corporate financial performance. *Social Responsibility Journal, 15*(1), 11–27. https://doi.org/10.1108/SRJ-11-2017-0254

Liern, V., & Pérez-Gladish, B. (2018). Ranking corporate sustainability: A flexible multidimensional approach based on linguistic variables. *International Transactions in Operational Research, 25*(3), 1081–1100. https://doi.org/10.1111/itor.12469

Lombardi, R. (2021). The going-concern in accounting research. In *The going-concern-principle in non-financial disclosure. SIDREA series in accounting and business administration*. Springer. https://doi.org/10.1007/978-3-030-81127-3_1

Luo, X., Wang, H., Raithel, S., & Zheng, Q. (2015). Corporate social performance, analyst stock recommendations, and firm future returns. *Strategic Management Journal, 36*(1), 123–136. https://doi.org/10.1002/smj.2219

Maas, K., Schaltegger, S., & Crutzen, N. (2016). Integrating corporate sustainability assessment, management accounting, control, and reporting. *Journal of Cleaner Production, 136*, 237–248. https://doi.org/10.1016/j.jclepro.2016.05.008

Mahoney, L. S., Thorne, L., Cecil, L., & LaGore, W. (2013). A research note on standalone corporate social responsibility reports: Signaling or greenwashing? *Critical Perspectives on Accounting, 24*(4–5), 350–359. https://doi.org/10.1016/j.cpa.2012.09.008

Maniora, J. (2017). Is integrated reporting really the superior mechanism for the integration of ethics into the Core business model? An empirical analysis. *Journal of Business Ethics, 140*(4), 755–786. https://doi.org/10.1007/s10551-015-2874-z

Martin-Sardesai, A., & Guthrie, J. (2020). Social report innovation: Evidence from a major Italian bank 2007–2012. *Meditari Accountancy Research, 28*(1), 72–88. https://doi.org/10.1108/MEDAR-10-2018-0383

Mathews, M. R. (1997). Twenty-five years of social and environmental accounting research: Is there a silver jubilee to celebrate? *Accounting, Auditing & Accountability Journal, 10*(4), 481–531. https://doi.org/10.1108/EUM0000000004417

Mathews, M. R., & Perera, M. H. B. (1996). Accounting theory and development. .

Moldan, B., & Dahl, A. (2012). Challenges to sustainability indicators T. In T. Hák, B. Moldan, & A. L. Dahl (Eds.), *Sustainability indicators: A scientific assessment* (pp. 1–26). Island Press.

Papoutsi, A., & Sodhi, M. M. S. (2020). Does disclosure in sustainability reports indicate actual sustainability performance? *Journal of Cleaner Production, 260*, 121049. https://doi.org/10.1016/j.jclepro.2020.121049

Paris, A. (2003). Il ruolo del rendiconto etico-ambientale nel sistema della comunicazione ambientale. *Cedam.*

Parker, L. D. (2005). Social and environmental accountability research: A view from the commentary box. *Accounting, Auditing and Accountability Journal, 18*(6), 842–860. https://doi.org/10.1108/09513570510627739

Pistoni, A., Songini, L., & Bavagnoli, F. (2018). Integrated reporting quality: An empirical analysis. *Corporate Social Responsibility and Environmental Management, 25*(4), 489–507. https://doi.org/10.1002/csr.1474

Puntillo, P. (2008). Il bilancio ambientale., *FabbricaVerde.*

Qiu, Y., Yin, S., & Wang, Y. D. (2016). Peer effects and voluntary green building certification. *Sustainability, 8*(7), 1–15. https://doi.org/10.3390/su8070632

Rahdari, A. H., & Anvary Rostamy, A. A. (2015). Designing a general set of sustainability indicators at the corporate level. *Journal of Cleaner Production, 108*, 757–771. https://doi.org/10.1016/j.jclepro.2015.05.108

Reid, J., & Rout, M. (2020). Developing sustainability indicators–the need for radical transparency. *Ecological Indicators, 110*, 105941. https://doi.org/10.1016/j.ecolind.2019.105941

Rija, M., & Tenuta, P. (2010). L'etica e la responsabilità sociale delle imprese nella teoria e nel business reale. *FrancoAngeli.*

Romolini, A. (2006). Il Bilancio di sostenibilità, Mulazzani, M., I servizi pubblici locali di distribuzione del gas. *FrancoAngeli.*

Rubino, F. E., Rija, M., Bronzetti, G., Sicoli, G., & Tenuta, P. (2016). An innovative model for a sustainability report in no-profit organizations. *International Journal of Learning and Intellectual Capital, 13*(2/3), 119–134. https://doi.org/10.1504/IJLIC.2016.075696

Rubino, F. (2007). Il bilancio sociale nelle aziende pubbliche locali, *Centro editoriale e librario dell'Università della Calabria.*

Rusconi, G. (2006). *Il bilancio sociale: economia, etica e responsabilità sociale dell'impresa*. Ediesse.

Rzeźnik, A., Hanley, K. W., & Pelizzon, L. (2021). Investor reliance on ESG ratings and stock Price performance. *SSRN Electronic Journal, 310.*

Sachs, J. D. (2012). From millennium development goals to sustainable development goals. *The Lancet, 379*(9832), 2206–2211. https://doi.org/10.1016/S0140-6736(12)60685-0

Scalet, S., & Kelly, T. F. (2010). CSR rating agencies: What is their global impact? *Journal of Business Ethics, 94*(1), 69–88. https://doi.org/10.1007/s10551-009-0250-6

Schreck, P., & Raithel, S. (2018). Corporate social performance, firm size, and organizational visibility: Distinct and joint effects on voluntary sustainability reporting. *Business and Society, 57*(4), 742–778. https://doi.org/10.1177/0007650315613120

Searcy, C. (2012). Corporate sustainability performance measurement systems: A review and research agenda. *Journal of Business Ethics, 107*(3), 239–253. https://doi.org/10.1007/s10551-011-1038-z

Semenova, N., & Hassel, L. G. (2015). On the validity of environmental performance metrics. *Journal of Business Ethics, 132*(2), 249–258. https://doi.org/10.1007/s10551-014-2323-4

Stirling, A. (1999). The appraisal of sustainability: Some problems and possible responses. *Local Environment, 4*(2), 111–135. https://doi.org/10.1080/13549839908725588

Tenuta, P. (2009). Indici e modelli di sostenibilità. *FrancoAngeli.*

Tettamanzi, P., Venturini, G., & Murgolo, M. (2022). Sustainability and financial accounting: A critical review on the ESG dynamics. *Environmental Science and Pollution Research, 29*, 16758–16761. https://doi.org/10.1007/s11356-022-18596-2

UK HM Treasury (2021) *UK welcomes work to develop global sustainability reporting standards alongside 40 international partners*. Gov.uk.

Unerman, J. (2008). Strategic reputation risk management and corporate social responsibility reporting. *Accounting, Auditing and Accountability Journal, 21*(3), 362–364. https://doi.org/10.1108/09513570810863941

Vaccari, A. (2005). Dal bilancio sociale al bilancio di sostenibilità, *Forum PA2005.*

Veltri, S., & Silvestri, A. (2015). The Free State university integrated reporting: A critical consideration. *Journal of Intellectual Capital, 16*(2), 443–462. https://doi.org/10.1108/JIC-06-2014-0077

Veltri, S., & Silvestri, A. (2020). The value relevance of corporate financial and nonfinancial information provided by the integrated report: A systematic review. *Business Strategy and the Environment, 29*(8), 3038–3054. https://doi.org/10.1002/bse.2556

Venturelli, A., Caputo, F., Cosma, S., Leopizzi, R., & Pizzi, S. (2017). Directive 2014/95/EU: Are Italian companies already compliant? *Sustainability, 9*(8). https://doi.org/10.3390/su9081385

Vitolla, F., Raimo, N., & Rubino, M. (2019a). Appreciations, criticisms, determinants, and effects of integrated reporting: A systematic literature review. *Corporate Social Responsibility and Environmental Management, 26*(2), 518–528. https://doi.org/10.1002/csr.1734

Vitolla, F., Raimo, N., Rubino, M., & Garzoni, A. (2019b). The impact of national culture on integrated reporting quality. A stakeholder theory approach. *Business Strategy and the Environment, 28*(8), 1558–1571. https://doi.org/10.1002/bse.2332

Wahl, A., Charifzadeh, M., & Diefenbach, F. (2020). Voluntary adopters of integrated reporting–evidence on forecast accuracy and firm value. *Business Strategy and the Environment, 29*(6), 2542–2556. https://doi.org/10.1002/bse.2519

Wang, Q., Dou, J., & Jia, S. (2016). A meta-analytic review of corporate social responsibility and corporate financial performance: The moderating effect of contextual factors. *Business and Society, 55*(8), 1083–1121. https://doi.org/10.1177/0007650315584317

Wilmshurst, T. D., & Frostr, G. R. (2000). Corporate environmental reporting: A test of legitimacy theory. *Accounting Auditing & Accountability Journal, 13*(1), 10–26.

# Chapter 4
# Corporate Sustainability and Financial Performance

**Abstract** In the third chapter, we empirically verify the impact of Corporate Sustainability (CS), measured through ESG rates, on Corporate Financial Performance (CFP) in family and nonfamily firms. Furthermore, the empirical analysis examines the moderating role of collegial leadership, a board characteristic that occurs when several executive members sit on the board of directors, on the link between firm sustainability and company performance. The work refers to the total sample of Italian companies listed on FTSE-MIB, the largest market dedicated to the most Italian capitalized companies, for the years 2015–2019. Our findings regarding the whole sample of firms show that CS rates do not affect the financial performance of Italian FTSE-MIB companies. By looking at the different ownership structures (family firms vs nonfamily firms), the econometric analyses indicate that higher CS rates are negatively associated with family firms' performance. The chapter concludes by showing that the negative relationship within family firm subsamples is positively moderated by the presence of more executive members on the board of directors of family companies.

## 1 Introduction

Empirical studies on the relationship between the sustainability of a company and its financial performance provide conflicting results (Aboulamer, 2018), leaving room for further investigation. In most cases, a positive correlation was highlighted (Alareeni & Hamdan, 2020; Jang et al., 2019; Chijoke-Mgbame et al., 2019; Chen & Wang, 2011). Other studies find a negative relationship (Brammer et al., 2006; Seifert et al., 2003) or the absence of a significant relationship (Martin Curran & Moran, 2007; Surroca et al., 2010).

The different results are often related to measuring sustainability performance (Endrikat et al., 2014; Horváthová, 2010; Wang et al., 2016). According to Hussain et al. (2018), the confusion in the relationship between sustainability and financial performance stems from the fact that third-party employ self-defined. Furthermore, much of the research focuses on the US market, and only a few examinations have been conducted on European markets (Friede et al., 2015; Nuber et al., 2020).

© The Author(s), under exclusive license to Springer Nature Switzerland AG 2022

P. Tenuta, D. R. Cambrea, *Corporate Sustainability*, SIDREA Series in Accounting and Business Administration, https://doi.org/10.1007/978-3-031-11491-5_4

Therefore, given the uncertainty and discrepancy of the inconclusive results in the literature (Sekhon & Kathuria, 2019), the primary objective of this research is to verify the existence of a significant relationship between the level of sustainability and the financial performance of family and nonfamily Italian listed firms.

The issue of family businesses, on the other hand, has been much debated in relation to financial performance but not in terms of sustainability performance. In this vein, García-Ramos and García-Olalla (2011) noted that corporate governance topics, ownership issues, and CEO succession received the most attention from researchers investigating family businesses. On the contrary, relevant themes such as ethics and corporate social responsibility have received less attention.

There are numerous reports in the literature about the need to feed studies on the link between family businesses and sustainability performance. According to Adomako et al. (2019), the "question of whether family businesses are more sustainably oriented than nonfamily businesses remains largely unanswered." In the same way, Broccardo et al. (2019) highlighted the lack of corporate sustainability studies in family businesses (Berrone et al., 2010; Debicki et al., 2009). Martínez-Ferrero and Frías-Aceituno (2015) believe that the issue of sustainability in family businesses is significantly under-researched and, consequently, future research could analyze conceptual and empirical aspects and verify their orientation towards sustainability issues. Benavides-Velasco et al. (2011) argue that current studies on the subject need to be stepped up. Despite the numerous studies in the literature, few empirical researchers examine family businesses (Broccardo et al., 2019), especially in some contexts where they are the vast majority of companies listed on the stock exchange (García-Ramos & García-Olalla, 2011; Acquaah, 2013; Chrisman et al., 2014; Singal & Gerde, 2015). In this regard, there are numerous reports in the literature about the need to feed studies on the link between family businesses and sustainability performance (Adomako et al., 2019; Broccardo et al., 2019). Therefore, although recent years have been characterized by greater attention on these topics, it is essential to proceed with further investigations (Campopiano & De Massis, 2015; Caputo et al., 2016; Kallmuenzer et al., 2018), which justifies our interest in this part of the research. Researchers and practitioners have applied various methods and techniques to investigate these relationships, but the results remain equivocal in the relationship between sustainability performance and financial performance or incomplete for family businesses. Our study aims to fill this gap using a recognized measurement of sustainability performance already used by other researchers (Landi et al., 2019; Landi & Sciarelli, 2019; Provasi & Harasheh, 2021; Sciarelli et al., 2019).

For 5 years from 2015 to 2019 we investigated the 40 companies of the Milan Exchange (FTSE-MIB 40 index, which includes the most capitalized listed companies in Italy). Companies are interested in being part of a sustainability index because it allows them to advertise the results achieved by increasing their reputation (Charlo et al., 2015). Analyzing the Italian market is a choice dictated by a context certainly suitable for testing our research hypotheses, given the significant presence of family businesses that have been subject to interesting analyses in the last year that analyze or suggest new studies on the subject (Provasi & Harasheh, 2021; Veltri et al., 2021).

We find that the relationship between sustainability and financial performance is not statistically significant in our total sample of analyses. On the other hand, distinguishing between family and nonfamily firms, the relationship becomes negative when only family firms are considered. This negative and statistically significant relationship in family businesses is positively moderated by collegial leadership (more board members with executive power).

The use of a sustainability index of companies listed on the FTSE-MIB for the entire period made available by the Standard Ethics rating company avoids the use of non-homogeneous criteria found in the literature review. Standard Ethics differs from other rating agencies because it follows a stakeholder-oriented approach and is based on each company's public documents. That index is inspired by the principles and guidelines of the European Union, the OECD, and the United Nations, ensuring the lack of subjective interpretations regarding CSR and CS ability definitions (Landi & Sciarelli, 2019).

Our research contributes to the existing literature and fills the gaps in the analysis relating to family businesses. Furthermore, distinguishing between family and nonfamily firms helps to increase research by revealing the role of the diversity of the board of directors in family businesses and adds an essential element neglected in previous studies, such as the possibility of having more subjects at the top decision-making (co-leadership, a typical feature of Italian family businesses).

However, the analysis has limitations. Results are limited to a specific country and period. Furthermore, the results may depend on the definitions of family businesses that are dissimilar to those used in the study. Future research should integrate the sample analysis of companies in multiple countries, looking at other variables of the board of directors such as gender diversity, age of women, educational qualifications, and CEO duality. Finally, future empirical works could consider alternative definitions of the family firm to verify whether the moderating role played by family control is according to the different degrees of family involvement in firms.

## 2 Literature Review and Research Hypotheses

### *2.1 Sustainability Performance and Financial Performance*

The relationship between corporate sustainability and financial performance has been the subject of numerous analyses from different theoretical perspectives (Lu & Taylor, 2018; Margolis & Walsh, 2003; Ruf et al., 2001), which gave different results.

Hussain et al. (2018), analyzing the relationship between sustainability performance and financial performance, distinguish the supporters of the neoclassical school ("traditionalist view") according to which sustainability initiatives impose additional costs (Hamilton, 1995), supporters of the "revisionist view" (Porter & van der Linde, 1995) according to which such initiatives improve financial performance and social well-being, researchers who recognize an inverse U-shaped relationship (Misani & Pogutz, 2015; Nuber et al., 2020).

Yet, numerous scholars seem to agree that "sustainability performance offers companies opportunities that, when managed strategically, could improve the financial performance of these companies through reputation creation" (Khattak, 2021). Wang et al. (2014) believe that sustainable business practices positively affect several factors, which, in turn, have positive consequences on business performance.

Charlo et al. (2015) show that Spanish companies, included in the FTSE4Good IBEX index, obtain higher returns on the market. According to the authors, being socially responsible does not harm the interests of investors as the profits obtained by these companies are no less than those obtained by companies classified as not socially responsible. Kurapatskie and Darnall (2013) examine the economic returns associated with the two types of sustainability activities derived from the framework of Hart and Milstein (2003) and find that the financial benefits associated with the higher-order sustainability activities of firms outweigh the financial benefits associated with lower-order sustainability activities.

Wagner and Blom (2011) analyzed the link between financial performance and the level of sustainability measured through the environmental management system (EMS) in 497 British and German companies. They find that the level of sustainability of a company is positively associated with the financial performance of financially well-performing companies and negatively with the results of less good companies. The EMS index has a positive influence on the financial results of good companies and a negative influence on the financial results of bad companies.

Despite the uncertainty arising from previous studies, Busch and Friede (2018), through a review of 25 meta-analyses, found a strong positive and bilateral relationship between social benefits (ecological or social) and the financial performance of companies.

Using a curvilinear approach, several studies explain the relationship between sustainability and financial performance (Adegbite et al., 2019; Trumpp & Guenther, 2017). The quadratic curvilinear impact can be convex (U-shaped) or concave (inversely U-shaped). Most previous studies find a non-inverted U-shaped relationship (Nuber et al., 2020).

According Barnett & Salomon, 2006 low levels of sustainability produce costs that exceed benefits, while high levels of sustainability produce benefits exceeding costs that positively impact financial performance. Trumpp and Guenther (2017), in their analysis, provide evidence of a "TLGT (too much of a good thing effect)," which indicates the type of relationship (positive, negative) is determined by the level of performance. More precisely, there is a negative relationship between environmental performance and financial performance for companies with a low level of environmental performance and a positive association for companies with a high level of environmental performance. This creates misaligned results that hinder generalizability (Bassetti et al., 2021).

Although most researchers find a positive link between sustainability and financial performance, several factors still cause uncertainty in the results (Fahad & Busru, 2021; Alareeni & Hamdan, 2020; Sahut et al., 2019). Numerous studies suggest that uneven sustainability performance measures are one of the main causes of the equivocal results (Endrikat et al., 2014; Horváthová, 2010; Lu et al., 2014).

This study supports the existence of a relationship between sustainability performance and financial performance consistent with the stakeholder theory. Given the uncertainty of the results, the topic continues to be the subject of extensive discussion and stimulates our first following research hypothesis.

*H1: There is a positive relationship between the level of sustainability and the financial performance of the company.*

## 2.2 Sustainability Performance and Financial Performance in Family and Nonfamily Firms

The sustainability literature has focused on how sustainability performance affects company performance without analyzing in-depth how this relationship differs across different types of companies. Despite the numerous researches that have been taking place in recent years, focusing on family businesses, the relationship is not clear between sustainability and financial performance and how this differs in family and nonfamily businesses.

López-Pérez et al. (2018) believe it is necessary to consider the socio-emotional wealth (SEW) approach in investigating family firms. The engagement in social responsibility activities of family firms can be analyzed through the socio-emotional wealth (SEW) theory (Cruz et al., 2014), according to which family companies are not exclusively interested in economic benefits deriving from the performance of business activities, but are also encouraged towards objectives linked to their socio-emotional sphere (Berrone et al., 2012; Gómez-Mejía et al., 2007). SEW supporters suggest that family business members are more likely to engage in social practices in search of a socio-emotional reward, even when there is no evidence of subsequent positive economic impacts (Berrone et al., 2012).

According to Broccardo et al. (2019), family businesses are generally more interested than nonfamily businesses in pursuing non-economic goals (Campopiano & De Massis, 2015; Chrisman et al., 2012; Kotlar & De Massis, 2013) aimed at sustainable development (Herrera & de las Heras-Rosas, 2020). They, therefore, tend to preserve their socio-emotional wealth, which is a complementary non-economic utility to economic wealth (Battaglia et al., 2016). Family businesses have peculiar characteristics such as the conservation (Chen et al., 2021), development and transfer of their legacy (Hirigoyen & Poulain-Rehm, 2014), and for these reasons, they are oriented toward long-term profit-seeking (Antheaume et al., 2013). In these contexts, the company is often seen as a vehicle for achieving continuity by fueling the future of the family (Rees & Rodionova, 2015) in terms of providing jobs, security, and income for the next generation (Miller et al., 2009). A long-time horizon directs long-term investments, such as sustainability practices (Memili et al., 2018).

From a theoretical point of view, family businesses will be more oriented towards socially responsible aspects than purely economic objectives (Block & Wagner, 2014; Cui et al., 2018). Therefore, we expect that in line with the SEW approach, family firms may be more focused on promoting a sustainable approach than nonfamily firms and that this may negatively impact financial performance.

Based on these considerations, we posit our second research hypothesis.

*H2: There is a negative relationship between the level of sustainability and the corporate financial performance of family businesses.*

## 2.3 Collegial Leadership

Academic researchers highlight the need to consider the heterogeneity of family businesses (Chua et al., 2012). The concept that family companies are all the same is mainly outdated and, consequently, makes it appropriate to study how the different peculiarities of family firms affect sustainability outcomes (Marques et al., 2014).

Some specific characteristics of the family businesses, such as the involvement of family members in managerial activities, as well as the cohabitation of various generations in the board or the participation of the founder in management activities, have already been extensively studied in the literature, both as regards it concerns their impact on corporate performance and their relationships with sustainability practices.

Le Breton-Miller and Miller (2016) propose some moderating contingencies in the governance structures, which can pursue positive sustainability practices. According to these authors, the governance factor that has the greatest impact on the social responsibility of family businesses is represented by the presence of family members on the board of directors. Similarly, Cabrera-Suárez and Martín-Santana (2015) show that companies with high family involvement, in which family members hold at least 50% of the governance and management positions, tend to have a higher level of sustainability. When the family is involved both in terms of ownership and in terms of management, it positively influences the social responsibility of the company (Canavati, 2018) and this influence increases if the family members are numerously represented within the management and in the board of directors (López-González et al., 2019).

Previous studies found greater efforts to ensure sustainability practices when the family is fully involved in the business (Chrisman et al., 2005). This is because family members, in the perspective of socio-emotional wealth, seem to be the main argument for greater engagement in sustainability (Chen et al., 2008), maintaining a significantly more responsible approach compared to non-FF (Walls et al., 2012). Similarly, Venturelli et al. (2021) find that companies with greater family control and larger size tend to engage more in sustainability behavior. Other empirical analyses show that family firms pursue more environmentally focused activities and household owners tend to be more environmentally focused when they control the business (Berrone et al., 2010).

According to Block and Wagner (2014), the presence of family members on the board of directors has a significant impact on corporate social responsibility performance. Furthermore, family members' presence emphasizes the desire not to dilute corporate control and preserve socio-emotional wealth (Gomez-Mejia et al., 2011). Many family members on the board of directors create an environmentally friendly company and active towards CSR (López-González et al., 2019).

Diversely from the research mentioned above, we aim to introduce collegial leadership as a new moderating factor that could drive family firms towards more profitable sustainability practices, allowing the companies to improve their financial and sustainability performance.

Collegial leadership among family members is a phenomenon that often occurs in family businesses (Cirillo et al., 2015). Sharing leadership, in terms of Co-CEOs, can be defined as a condition in which "executives perform the best work together and in a coordinated way, and are held jointly responsible for the results of the company" (Alvarez et al., 2007).

Several scholars have argued for a positive relationship between shared leadership and management team performance (Carson et al., 2007). It has been considered an intangible resource that encourages the sharing of information and intensifies the commitment made by executives (Carson et al., 2007). Sharing leadership allows the company to have wider knowledge and skills from multiple subjects (Alvarez et al., 2007). These skills facilitate greater creativity and greater rigor in the evaluation phases of strategic choices. Such a leadership structure gives the company more alternatives in the style of command, improving the approach to the different situations and interests of the various stakeholders (Alvarez et al., 2007; Arnone & Stumpf, 2010). In the case of Co-CEOs, compensation is made between the backgrounds and expertise of each CEO (Arena et al., 2011) and this could be more desirable when the complexity of the conditions requires broader skills (O'Toole et al., 2002). This governance structure appears to act as an additional or alternative monitoring mechanism exercised by the board of directors. This monitoring is mutually exercised between the Co-CEOs (Kandel & Lazear, 1992), making incentive mechanisms less necessary to reduce agency costs (Arena et al., 2011). Therefore, the Co-CEO seems to bring positive effects on better performance and business value.

The altruism and collectivism that characterize family members involved in management (Jaskiewicz & Klein, 2007; Kellermanns & Eddleston, 2004) favor, in addition to collaboration, also a franker communication by the relationship existing family member (Bubolz, 2001; Daily & Dollinger, 1992). The same altruism, in association with the greater participation of these members in the decision-making phases (an aspect underlying behavioral integration), seems to intensify the sharing of knowledge, the exchange of information and foster a greater sense of loyalty towards the company (Eddleston & Kellermanns, 2007; Kellermanns & Eddleston, 2004).

These arguments suggest a positive moderating effect deriving from collegial leadership on the board. Thus, we posit the following hypothesis.

*H3: Collegial leadership positively moderates the impact of sustainability on financial performance in family businesses.*

# 3 Methodology

## 3.1 Data Collection and Sample

We constructed our sample by combining and matching data from various databases. First, we obtained the ESG rate of 40 Italian firms listed at the Milan Exchange FTSE-MIB 40 index for 2015–2019. Second, we employed a unique hand-collected dataset to investigate our research hypotheses, which contains information on the board of directors' demographic and personal characteristics. Data were collected manually by referring to the annual reports on corporate governance of the individual firms, available on the official websites of the companies and the website of the Italian Stock Exchange. Finally, we merged the ESG data and governance dataset with the financial control variables provided by Datastream. The intersection of these data sets a final sample of 160 firm-year observations.

## 3.2 Dependent Variable

The dependent variable in the empirical models is performance, which was assessed using return on assets (ROA), defined as operating income divided by total assets (Lu & Herremans, 2019). This accounting measure is commonly used to analyze firm performance, including family firm performance (Wagner et al., 2015).

## 3.3 Independent and Moderating Variables

The main independent variable is *ESG Rate*, provided by Standard Ethics (www.standardethics.eu). Standard Ethics is an independent sustainability-rating agency that aims to promote sustainability and corporate governance principles (Landi & Sciarelli, 2019; Rossi & Harjoto, 2020). *ESG rate* measures the commitment and effectiveness of a company towards reducing environmental emissions in the production and operational processes. The existence of a sustainability index of listed companies makes it possible to identify socially responsible companies, avoiding the use of non-homogeneous criteria found in the review of the literature on the measurement of aspects of good social practices (Charlo et al., 2015).

The score ranges between EEE and F, where EEE indicated full compliance to the guidelines and recommendations on governance, sustainability, and ESG disclosure measures. Diversely, F represented the lowest level of compliance and suggested an inability to manage sustainability. Following previous literature (Landi & Sciarelli, 2019; Rossi & Harjoto, 2020), we converted the alphabetical letters into numerical values that represent the non-financial disclosures rating of a firm (ESGRATE), where EEE = 9, EEE − = 8, EE+ = 7, EE = 6, EE − = 5, E+ = 4, E = 3, E− = 2, F = 1, or zero if a company does not have an SER rating.

Consistent with previous studies (Miller et al., 2013), we identified *family firms* (also denoted as *FFs*) as those firms where one or two closely related families control at least 25% of the shares (Minichilli et al., 2016). *Collegial leadership* is a continuous variable that accounts for the presence of a co-leadership structure on the board of directors. It has been computed as the ratio of executive members to board size.

## 3.4 Control Variables

We included several financial and governance variables as controls in all regressions. *Firm size* is measured as the natural logarithm of total assets (Orazalin & Baydauletov, 2020). *Debt* was calculated as the ratio of long-term debt to total assets (Lepore et al., 2018). *Cash holdings* is the ratio of cash and cash equivalents to net assets (Wu et al., 2017). We also employed as control variables *Board size*, which is measured as the number of members of the board of directors (Furlotti et al., 2018), and *Independent directors*, computed by the ratio of independent directors on the board (Cucari et al., 2018). *CEO duality* was coded as a dummy variable that took a value of one when the CEO was also the chairperson of the board and took a value of zero otherwise (Romano et al., 2020). Finally, we considered *Female directors*, computed as the percentage of female directors on the board (Cambrea et al., 2019).

## 3.5 Model

To test the research hypotheses empirically, we estimate the following empirical model:

$$\begin{aligned} ROA_{\mathrm{i},t} = {} & ESG\ Rate_{\mathrm{i},t} + ESG\ Rate_{\mathrm{i}\ \mathrm{i},t} \times Family\ firms_{\mathrm{i},t} + ESG\ Rate_{\mathrm{i}\ \mathrm{i},t} \\ & \times Family\ firm_{\mathrm{i},t} \times Collegial\ leadership_{\mathrm{i},t} + Control\ variables_{\mathrm{i},t-1} \\ & + Year_t + Industry_i + \varepsilon_{\mathrm{i},t} \end{aligned}$$

where $i$ indexes firms and $t$ is a yearly time index, $Year_t$ and $Industry_i$ capture the year and industry effects respectively, and $\varepsilon_{i,t}$ is the random disturbance. The research hypotheses are tested by using ordinary least squares (OLS) regressions and heteroscedasticity-adjusted standard errors. This econometric methodology has been adopted in several empirical studies that investigate the effects of board diversity on environmental, social, and governance (ESG) (Amore et al., 2019; Katmon et al., 2019).

We are aware that a different econometric approach, such as fixed effects or random effects, could be more suitable considering the longitudinal structure of our dataset, which is similar to a panel data structure. However, we realize that in our dataset, the variation of the Standard Ethics Rating is none or very minimal. In the presence of a dataset suffering from slowly changing variables, the fixed effects or random effects estimates could be not efficient (Plümper & Troeger, 2007). Therefore, we opted to apply an OLS regression.

# 4 Analysis and Results

## *4.1 Descriptive Analysis*

Table 4.1 presents two panels of descriptive information for our sample of firms. Panel A provides means, medians, standard deviations, and first and third quartiles for all the variables in our sample. Panel B shows the results of the difference of means tests between family and nonfamily firms.

Panel A of Table 4.1 shows the main statistics for the entire sample of firms. The data shows that, on average, the CEO is also the board's chairman in 11.5% of cases. The average percentage of independent directors on the boards is almost 58%. The average number of board members is very close to 12, indicating that Italian companies listed at FTSE-MIB tend to adopt bigger boards than the other Italian listed companies, which have a board comprised of 9–10 members (Rubino et al., 2017). Finally, the presence of the female gender represents approximately 32% of the total directors. This percentage has increased considerably because of Law 120/2011 on gender quotas, which required women on the boards of Italian listed firms. Family firms represent, on average, 37% of the total companies.

Table 4.2 reports the correlation among the variables used in the econometric analysis.

## *4.2 Hypotheses Testing*

We test our propositions using OLS regression analysis with year and industry fixed effects. Regression results are presented in Table 4.3.

Model 1 of Table 4.3 provides the results for Hypothesis 1, which predicted that a higher *ESG Rate* improves the firm performance. The coefficient for our main independent variable ($\beta = -0.004$), *ESG rate*, is not statistically significant

**Table 4.1** Descriptive statistics

Panel A: Descriptive statistics for the full sample

| Variables | Mean | Standard Deviation | 25th Percentile | Median | 75th Percentile |
|---|---|---|---|---|---|
| ROA | 0.060 | 0.066 | 0.014 | 0.044 | 0.070 |
| ESG rate | 4.680 | 1.428 | 3.000 | 5.000 | 6.000 |
| Family firms | 0.371 | 0.484 | 0.000 | 0.000 | 1.000 |
| Collegial leadership | 0.204 | 0.162 | 0.111 | 0.133 | 0.273 |
| Firm size | 23.834 | 1.814 | 22.518 | 23.678 | 25.222 |
| Debt | 0.197 | 0.147 | 0.078 | 0.175 | 0.304 |
| Cash holdings | 0.115 | 0.098 | 0.037 | 0.099 | 0.155 |
| Board size | 11.923 | 3.826 | 9.000 | 11.000 | 15.000 |
| CEO duality | 0.115 | 0.319 | 0.000 | 0.000 | 0.000 |
| Independent directors | 0.577 | 0.167 | 0.533 | 0.583 | 0.667 |
| Female directors | 0.322 | 0.096 | 0.294 | 0.333 | 0.368 |

**Panel B: Comparison of family and nonfamily firms**

| | **Variables** | **Family firms** | **Nonfamily firms** | **Difference** | **t-statistic** |
|---|---|---|---|---|---|
| **Number of firm-years** | | **62** | **98** | | |
| 1 | ROA | 0.107 | 0.032 | 0.075*** | 9.15 |
| 2 | ESG rate | 3.492 | 5.387 | −1.895*** | −10.86 |
| 3 | Collegial leadership | 0.234 | 0.187 | 0.047* | 1.92 |
| 4 | Firm size | 22.666 | 24.523 | −1.857*** | −7.91 |
| 5 | Debt | 0.194 | 0.199 | −0.005 | 0.23 |
| 6 | Cash holdings | 0.174 | 0.080 | 0.094*** | 7.20 |
| 7 | Board size | 11.861 | 11.959 | −0.098 | 0.17 |
| 8 | CEO duality | 0.225 | 0.050 | 0.175*** | 3.81 |
| 9 | Independent directors | 0.513 | 0.620 | −0.107*** | −4.44 |
| 10 | Female directors | 0.297 | 0.337 | −0.040** | −2.87 |

Source: our elaboration

($p > 0.10$), thereby not supporting our hypothesis. Models 2 and 3 of Table 4.3 report the findings on the relationship between *ESG Rate* and firm performance within nonfamily and family firms, respectively. Regarding the primary independent variable of the research, for nonfamily firms, the coefficient of the variable *ESG rate* is not statistically significant ($\beta = -0.002, p < 0.10$). Differently, in the subsample of family firms, the variable *ESG rate* becomes negative and statistically significant ($\beta = -0.017$, $p < 0.05$). Thus, family companies with superior *ESG rate* are associated with a lower accounting-based performance. Because the interpretation of moderating effects can be challenging based solely on outcome tables, we graphically illustrate the relationship between *ESG rate* and ROA in the nonfamily and family subsamples (see Fig. 4.1).

Model 4 of Table 4.3 shows that our results are robust to including an interaction for *ESG rate* and the family firm dummy. Model 5 of Table 4.3 tests our third

**Table 4.2** Correlation matrix

| | Variables | 1 | 2 | 3 | 4 | 5 |
|---|---|---|---|---|---|---|
| 1 | ROA | 1 | | | | |
| 2 | ESG rate | −0.332$^{***}$ | 1 | | | |
| 3 | Family firms | 0.547$^{***}$ | −0.642$^{***}$ | 1 | | |
| 4 | Collegial leadership | 0.268$^{***}$ | −0.302$^{***}$ | 0.322$^{***}$ | 1 | |
| 5 | Firm size | −0.704$^{***}$ | 0.407$^{***}$ | −0.471$^{***}$ | −0.523$^{***}$ | 1 |
| 6 | Debt | 0.0390 | −0.261$^{**}$ | 0.0372 | −0.0523 | −0.0754 |
| 7 | Cash holdings | 0.605$^{***}$ | −0.227$^{**}$ | 0.548$^{***}$ | 0.127 | −0.413$^{***}$ |
| 8 | Board size | −0.255$^{**}$ | 0.00794 | −0.0693 | −0.116 | 0.341$^{***}$ |
| 9 | CEO duality | 0.372$^{***}$ | −0.233$^{**}$ | 0.310$^{***}$ | 0.0228 | −0.126 |
| 10 | Independent directors | −0.285$^{***}$ | 0.369$^{***}$ | −0.294$^{***}$ | −0.616$^{***}$ | 0.508$^{***}$ |
| 11 | Female directors | −0.188$^{*}$ | 0.209$^{**}$ | −0.303$^{***}$ | −0.204$^{*}$ | 0.186$^{*}$ |

| | Variables | 6 | 7 | 8 | 9 | 10 | 11 |
|---|---|---|---|---|---|---|---|
| 1 | ROA | | | | | | |
| 2 | ESG rate | | | | | | |
| 3 | Family firms | | | | | | |
| 4 | Collegial leadership | | | | | | |
| 5 | Firm size | | | | | | |
| 6 | Debt | 1 | | | | | |
| 7 | Cash holdings | 0.00228 | 1 | | | | |
| 8 | Board size | −0.237$^{**}$ | −0.329$^{***}$ | 1 | | | |
| 9 | CEO duality | −0.00945 | 0.390$^{***}$ | −0.0274 | 1 | | |
| 10 | Independent directors | 0.0641 | −0.0936 | 0.0727 | −0.198$^{*}$ | 1 | |
| 11 | Female directors | −0.0209 | −0.255$^{**}$ | −0.0979 | −0.224$^{**}$ | 0.250$^{**}$ | 1 |

$^{*}p < 0.05$, $^{**}p < 0.01$, $^{***}p < 0.001$
Source: our elaboration

hypothesis, suggesting that the presence of collegial leadership on the board positively moderates the relationship between ESG rate and a firm's performance. The coefficient of the three-way interaction between *ESG rate, family firms,* and *collegial leadership* is positive and statistically significant ($\beta = 0.154, p < 0.01$) and, thus, our Hypothesis 3 is fully supported.

Figure 4.2 presents a plot showing how firm performance is related to EGS rate under different shareholder (family vs nonfamily) and collegial leadership levels. Figure 4.2 indicates that ESG practices are more beneficial in family firms characterized by higher levels of collegial leadership.

**Table 4.3** Regression results

| | (1) | (2) | (3) | (4) | (5) |
|---|---|---|---|---|---|
| Variables | Full sample | Nonfamily firms | Family firms | Interaction | Interaction |
| ESG rate | −0.004 | −0.002 | **−0.017**** | 0.001 | 0.002 |
| | (0.173) | (0.318) | **(0.041)** | (0.782) | (0.654) |
| Family firms (FFs) | | | | 0.081** | 0.215*** |
| | | | | (0.023) | (0.000) |
| ESG rate*FFs | | | | **−0.017**** | **−0.041***** |
| | | | | **(0.037)** | **(0.001)** |
| Collegial leadership | | | | | 0.097 |
| | | | | | (0.440) |
| ESG rate*collegial leadership | | | | | −0.016 |
| | | | | | (0.495) |
| FFs*collegial leadership | | | | | −0.745*** |
| | | | | | (0.000) |
| ESG rate*FFs*collegial leadership | | | | | **0.154***** |
| | | | | | **(0.001)** |
| Firm size | −0.014*** | −0.004 | −0.027*** | −0.016*** | −0.017*** |
| | (0.001) | (0.200) | (0.000) | (0.000) | (0.000) |
| Debt | −0.129*** | 0.011 | −0.085 | −0.119*** | −0.132*** |
| | (0.000) | (0.739) | (0.109) | (0.000) | (0.000) |
| Cash holdings | 0.037 | 0.091** | 0.121* | 0.044 | 0.017 |
| | (0.321) | (0.023) | (0.080) | (0.245) | (0.628) |
| Board size | 0.001 | −0.000 | 0.004 | 0.001 | 0.001 |
| | (0.368) | (0.724) | (0.237) | (0.410) | (0.677) |
| CEO duality | 0.026** | 0.015 | 0.060*** | 0.015 | 0.012 |
| | (0.016) | (0.299) | (0.009) | (0.186) | (0.319) |
| Independent directors | 0.012 | 0.002 | 0.091 | 0.010 | 0.004 |
| | (0.571) | (0.899) | (0.166) | (0.623) | (0.836) |
| Female directors | 0.008 | −0.042 | 0.043 | 0.006 | −0.043 |
| | (0.838) | (0.182) | (0.707) | (0.889) | (0.259) |
| Constant | 0.381*** | 0.130** | 0.606*** | 0.400*** | 0.461*** |
| | (0.000) | (0.038) | (0.000) | (0.000) | (0.000) |
| Year dummies | Yes | Yes | Yes | Yes | Yes |
| Industry effects | Yes | Yes | Yes | Yes | Yes |
| Random effects | Yes | Yes | Yes | Yes | Yes |
| R-squared | 0.230 | 0.255 | 0.0922 | 0.210 | 0.374 |
| Number of id | 40 | 25 | 15 | 40 | 40 |
| Observations | 160 | 98 | 62 | 160 | 160 |

*pval in parentheses *** $p < 0.01$, ** $p < 0.05$, * $p < 0.1$*
Source: our elaboration

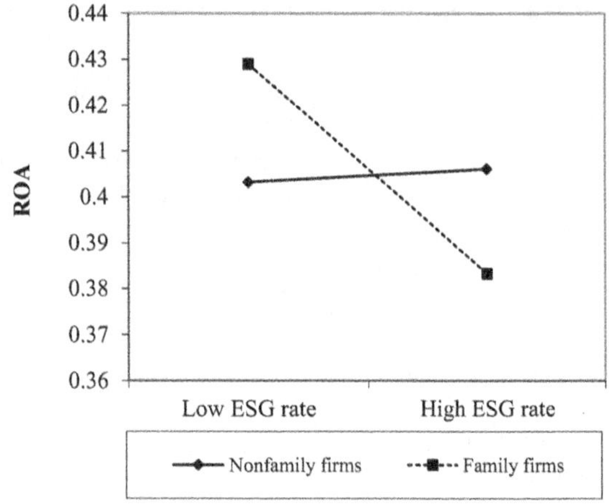


**Fig. 4.1** Effects of ESG rate within the family and nonfamily firms. Source: our elaboration

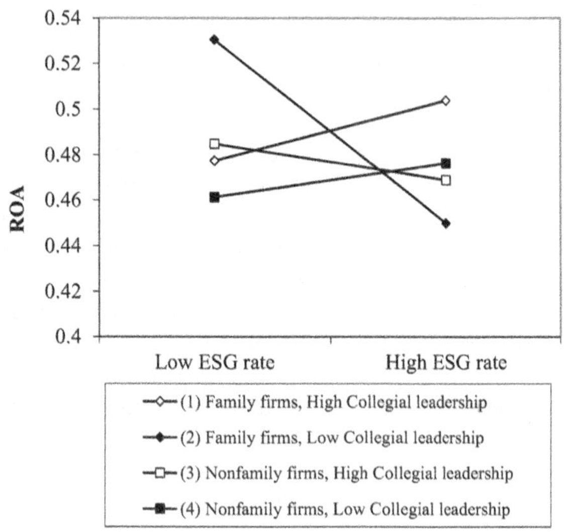


**Fig. 4.2** Moderating effect of collegial leadership on the relationship between ESG rate and ROA in family firms and nonfamily firms. Source: our elaboration

## 5 Discussion

This research contributes significantly to understanding a topical issue: the effects of sustainability practices, expressed in terms of ESG, on corporate performance. The growing interest of the world's major economies in the green economy, which must be in line with the expectations of corporate stakeholders and shareholders, is contributing substantially to increasing the debate in the academic and business community.

After testing the relationship between sustainability and firm performance across the sample under analysis, this paper aimed to test and investigate this relationship in family firms. Subsequently, the role of collegial leadership as a board-specific factor that can help to moderate the impact of sustainability practices on the book value of family firms was also analyzed.

The empirical analysis, conducted on a sample of 160 Italian listed companies from 2015 to 2019, showed a negative relationship between ESG rate and company performance. However, the introduction in the model of the interaction variable, referring to board-specific characteristics, highlights how the relationship between ESG rate and performance appears significantly conditioned by the presence of multiple directors with an executive role. The results appear attractive in providing a new interpretative key on the contrasting results concerning the link between investments in sustainability activities and performance in family businesses, as the effect on performance is moderated by the board of directors' characteristics. Specifically, this effect is particularly favorable in firms where multiple board members have executive power, a condition referred to as collegial leadership.

The firm's management by multiple individuals with executive powers leads to positive effects. Under the perspective of socio-emotional wealth, management is characterized by a high level of efficiency in this managerial condition. The presence of several directors with executive roles enables the board's professional background and human capital to be enhanced. Consequently, company management, which appears legitimized by the multiple components with executive roles, can take shared decisions, not risk making "risky" choices that could harm company results.

Naturally, this research has several limitations. First, although Italy is an interesting institutional context well suited to our empirical research, it is not sure that the same conclusions can be applied to different countries. Future research might consider extending these analyses to samples of firms across several countries. Second, the results may depend on the use of definitions of family firms that are dissimilar to those used in the study. Our work does not distinguish between family firms with active members in corporate management and those with no family members in key corporate governance roles. Therefore, future empirical work could consider alternative definitions of a family business in order to test whether the moderating role played by family control is determined by the different degrees of family involvement in firms.

The present work draws interesting implications for institutional actors who, with some vigor, have recommended the increase in sustainability activities and those who intend to invest in firms. The empirical results allow us to share companies' resistance towards greater investment in the green economy, as these investments do not seem to increase accounting performance in family businesses.

The conclusions reached by the study allow us to state that it is not enough to make investments in sustainability activities in order to have good management results. Therefore, institutional actors should examine all aspects of sustainability policies, taking into account, first of all, the various types and different configurations of businesses present on the market, but above all, considering the specific characteristics of the institutional context of reference before trying to influence the investment decisions of businesses. With regard to family firms, the study suggests that it is difficult for them to translate investments in sustainability into improved performance. However, the presence of multiple directors with an executive role is a safeguard for family shareholders, who may benefit from increased firm value. From this critical result comes the suggestion for family shareholders not to channel executive power into the hands of a single-family member but to share management duties among several board members, whether family members or not. This characteristic of family-controlled businesses, known as collegial leadership, enables family businesses to evaluate investment choices in sustainability activities more efficiently, increasing business performance and generating wealth for both the stakeholders of a company and its controlling shareholders.

## References

Aboulamer, A. (2018). Adopting a circular business model improves market equity value. *Thunderbird International Business Review, 60*(5), 765–769. https://doi.org/10.1002/tie.21922

Acquaah, M. (2013). Management control systems, business strategy and performance: A comparative analysis of family and non-family businesses in a transition economy in sub-Saharan Africa. *Journal of Family Business Strategy, 4*(2), 131–146. https://doi.org/10.1016/j.jfbs.2013.03.002

Adegbite, E., Guney, Y., Kwabi, F., & Tahir, S. (2019). Financial and corporate social performance in the UK listed firms: The relevance of non-linearity and lag effects. *Review of Quantitative Finance and Accounting, 52*(1), 105–158. https://doi.org/10.1007/s11156-018-0705-x

Adomako, S., Amankwah-Amoah, J., Danso, A., Konadu, R., & Owusu-Agyei, S. (2019). Environmental sustainability orientation and performance of family and nonfamily firms. *Business Strategy and the Environment, 28*(6), 1250–1259. https://doi.org/10.1002/bse.2314

Alareeni, B. A., & Hamdan, A. (2020). ESG impact on performance of US S&P 500-listed firms. *Corporate Governance: The International Journal of Business in Society., 20*(7), 1409–1428. https://doi.org/10.1108/CG-06-2020-0258

Alvarez, J. L., Svejenova, S., & Vives, L. (2007). Leading in pairs. *MIT Sloan Management Review, 48*(4), 48408.

Amore, M. D., Bennedsen, M., Larsen, B., & Rosenbaum, P. (2019). CEO education and corporate environmental footprint. *Journal of Environmental Economics and Management, 94*, 254–273. https://doi.org/10.1016/j.jeem.2019.02.001

Antheaume, N., Robic, P., & Barbelivien, D. (2013). French family business and longevity: Have they been conducting sustainable development policies before it became a fashion? *Business History, 55*(6), 942–962. https://doi.org/10.1080/00076791.2012.744583

Arena, M. P., Ferris, S. P., & Unlu, E. (2011). It takes two: The incidence and effectiveness of co-CEOs. *Financial Review, 46*(3), 385–412. https://doi.org/10.1111/j.1540-6288.2011.00305.x

Arnone, M., & Stumpf, S. A. (2010). Shared leadership: From rivals to co-CEOs. *Strategy and Leadership, 38*(2), 15–21. https://doi.org/10.1108/10878571011029019

Barnett, M. L., & Salomon, R. M. (2006). Beyond dichotomy: The curvilinear relationship between social responsibility and financial performance. *Strategic Management Journal, 27*(11), 1101–1122. https://doi.org/10.1002/smj.557

Bassetti, T., Blasi, S., & Sedita, S. R. (2021). The management of sustainable development: A longitudinal analysis of the effects of environmental performance on economic performance. *Business Strategy and the Environment, 30*(1), 21–37. https://doi.org/10.1002/bse.2607

Battaglia, M., Passetti, E., Bianchi, L., & Frey, M. (2016). Managing for integration: A longitudinal analysis of management control for sustainability. *Journal of Cleaner Production, 136*, 213–225. https://doi.org/10.1016/j.jclepro.2016.01.108

Benavides-Velasco, C. A., Quintana-García, C., & Guzmán-Parra, V. F. (2011). Trends in family business research. *Small Business Economics, 40*(1), 41–57. https://doi.org/10.1007/S11187-011-9362-3

Berrone, P., Cruz, C., & Gomez-Mejia, L. R. (2012). Socioemotional wealth in family firms: Theoretical dimensions, assessment approaches, and agenda for future research. *Family Business Review, 25*, 258–279. https://doi.org/10.1177/0894486511435355

Berrone, P., Cruz, C., Gomez-Mejia, L. R., & Larraza-Kintana, M. (2010). Socioemotional wealth and corporate responses to institutional pressures: Do family-controlled firms pollute less? *Administrative Science Quarterly, 55*(1), 82–113. https://doi.org/10.2189/asqu.2010.55.1.82

Block, J. H., & Wagner, M. (2014). The effect of family ownership on different dimensions of corporate social responsibility: Evidence from large US firms. *Business Strategy and the Environment, 23*(7), 475–492. https://doi.org/10.1002/bse.1798

Brammer, S., Brooks, C., & Pavelin, S. (2006). Corporate social performance and stock returns: UK evidence from disaggregate measures. *Financial Management, 35*(3), 97–116. https://doi.org/10.1111/j.1755-053X.2006.tb00149.x

Broccardo, L., Truant, E., & Zicari, A. (2019). Internal corporate sustainability drivers: What evidence from family firms? A literature review and research agenda. *Corporate Social Responsibility and Environmental Management, 26*(1), 1–18. https://doi.org/10.1002/csr.1672

Bubolz, M. M. (2001). Family as source, user, and builder of social capital. *The Journal of Socio-Economics, 30*(2), 129–131. https://doi.org/10.1016/s1053-5357(00)00091-3

Busch, T., & Friede, G. (2018). The robustness of the corporate social and financial performance relation: A second-order meta-analysis. *Corporate Social Responsibility and Environmental Management, 25*(4), 583–608. https://doi.org/10.1002/csr.1480

Cabrera-Suárez, M. K., & Martín-Santana, J. D. (2015). Board composition and performance in Spanish non-listed family firms: The influence of type of directors and CEO duality. *BRQ Business Research Quarterly, 18*(4), 213–229. https://doi.org/10.1016/j.brq.2014.08.001

Cambrea, D. R., Tenuta, P., & Vastola, V. (2019). Female directors and corporate cash holdings: Monitoring vs executive roles. *Management Decision, 58*(2), 295–312. https://doi.org/10.1108/MD-11-2018-1289

Campopiano, G., & De Massis, A. (2015). Corporate social responsibility reporting: A content analysis in family and non-family firms. *Journal of Business Ethics, 129*(3), 511–534. https://doi.org/10.1007/s10551-014-2174-z

Canavati, S. (2018). Corporate social performance in family firms: A meta-analysis. *Journal of Family Business Management, 8*(3), 235–273. https://doi.org/10.1108/JFBM-05-2018-0015

Caputo, A., Matteo Pellegrini, M., Dabic, M., & Paul Dana, L. (2016). Internationalisation of firms from central and Eastern Europe: A systematic literature review. *European Business Review, 28*(6), 630–651. https://doi.org/10.1108/EBR-01-2016-0004/FULL/HTML

Carson, J. B., Tesluk, P. E., & Marrone, J. A. (2007). Shared leadership in teams: An investigation of antecedent conditions and performance. *Academy of Management Journal, 50*(5), 1217–1234. https://doi.org/10.2307/20159921

Charlo, M. J., Moya, I., & Muñoz, A. M. (2015). Sustainable development and corporate financial performance: A study based on the FTSE4 good IBEX index. *Business Strategy and the Environment, 24*(4), 277–288. https://doi.org/10.1002/bse.1824

Chen, H., & Wang, X. (2011). Corporate social responsibility and corporate financial performance in China: An empirical research from Chinese firms. *Corporate Governance: The International Journal of Business in Society., 11*(4), 361–370. https://doi.org/10.1108/14720701111159217

Chen, S., Chen, X., & Cheng, Q. (2008). Do family firms provide more or less voluntary disclosure? *Journal of Accounting Research, 46*(3), 499–536. https://doi.org/10.1111/j.1475-679X.2008.00288.x

Chen, V. Z., Hobdari, B., Kellermanns, F. W., & Sluhan, A. (2021). For love or money? Family versus financial blockholders in international acquisitions. *Corporate Governance: An International Review., 1-21*. https://doi.org/10.1111/corg.12392

Chijoke-Mgbame, A. M., Mgbame, C. O., Akintoye, S., & Ohalehi, P. (2019). The role of corporate governance on CSR disclosure and firm performance in a voluntary environment. *Corporate Governance: The International Journal of Business in Society, 20*(2), 294–306. https://doi.org/10.1108/CG-06-2019-0184

Chrisman, J. J., Chua, J. H., & Steier, L. (2005). Sources and consequences of distinctive Familiness: An introduction. *Entrepreneurship Theory and Practice, 29*(3), 237–247. https://doi.org/10.1111/j.1540-6520.2005.00080.x

Chrisman, J. J., Chua, J. H., Pearson, A. W., & Barnett, T. (2012). Family involvement, family influence, and family-centered non-economic goals in small firms. *Entrepreneurship: Theory and Practice, 36*(2), 267–293. https://doi.org/10.1111/j.1540-6520.2010.00407.x

Chrisman, J. J., Memili, E., & Misra, K. (2014). Nonfamily managers, family firms, and the winner's curse: The influence of noneconomic goals and bounded rationality. *Entrepreneurship: Theory and Practice, 38*(5), 1103–1127. https://doi.org/10.1111/etap.12014

Chua, J. H., Chrisman, J. J., Steier, L. P., & Rau, S. B. (2012). Sources of heterogeneity in family firms: An introduction. *Entrepreneurship Theory and Practice, 36*(6), 1103–1113. https://doi.org/10.1111/j.1540-6520.2012.00540.x

Cirillo, A., Romano, M., & Pennacchio, L. (2015). All the power in two hands: The role of CEOs in family IPOs. *European Management Journal, 33*(5), 392–406. https://doi.org/10.1016/j.emj.2015.06.003

Cruz, C., Larraza-Kintana, M., Garcés-Galdeano, L., & Berrone, P. (2014). Are family firms really more socially responsible? *Entrepreneurship: Theory and Practice, 38*(6), 1295–1316. https://doi.org/10.1111/etap.12125

Cucari, N., Esposito De Falco, S., & Orlando, B. (2018). Diversity of Board of Directors and Environmental Social Governance: Evidence from Italian listed companies. *Corporate Social Responsibility and Environmental Management, 25*(3), 250–266. https://doi.org/10.1002/csr.1452

Cui, J., Jo, H., & Na, H. (2018). Does corporate social responsibility affect information asymmetry? *Journal of Business Ethics, 148*(3), 549–572. https://doi.org/10.1007/s10551-015-3003-8

Daily, C. M., & Dollinger, M. J. (1992). Empirical examination of family business.Pdf. *Family Business Review, 5*, 117–136.

Debicki, B. J., Matherne, C. F., Kellermanns, F. W., & Chrisman, J. J. (2009). Family business research in the new millennium. *Family Business Review, 22*(2), 151–166. https://doi.org/10.1177/0894486509333598

Eddleston, K. A., & Kellermanns, F. W. (2007). Destructive and productive family relationships: A stewardship theory perspective. *Journal of Business Venturing, 22*(4), 545–565. https://doi.org/10.1016/j.jbusvent.2006.06.004

Endrikat, J., Guenther, E., & Hoppe, H. (2014). Making sense of conflicting empirical findings: A meta-analytic review of the relationship between corporate environmental and financial performance. *European Management Journal, 32*(5), 735–751. https://doi.org/10.1016/j.emj.2013.12.004

Fahad, P., & Busru, S. A. (2021). CSR disclosure and firm performance: Evidence from an emerging market. *Corporate Governance: The International Journal of Business in Society., 21*(4), 553–568. https://doi.org/10.1108/CG-05-2020-0201

Friede, G., Busch, T., & Bassen, A. (2015). ESG and financial performance: Aggregated evidence from more than 2000 empirical studies. *Journal of Sustainable Finance and Investment, 5*(4), 210–233. https://doi.org/10.1080/20430795.2015.1118917

Furlotti, K., Mazza, T., Tibiletti, V., & Triani, S. (2018). Women in top positions on boards of directors: Gender policies disclosed in Italian sustainability reporting. *Corporate Social Responsibility and Environmental Management, 26*, 1–14. https://doi.org/10.1002/csr.1657

García-Ramos, R., & García-Olalla, M. (2011). Board characteristics and firm performance in public founder- and nonfounder-led family businesses. *Journal of Family Business Strategy, 2*(4), 220–231. https://doi.org/10.1016/j.jfbs.2011.09.001

Gomez-Mejia, L. R., Cruz, C., Berrone, P., & de Castro, J. (2011). The bind that ties: Socioemotional wealth preservation in family firms. *Academy of Management Annals, 5*, 653–707. https://doi.org/10.1080/19416520.2011.593320

Gómez-Mejía, L. R., Haynes, K. T., Núñez-Nickel, M., Jacobson, K. J. L., & Moyano-Fuentes, J. (2007). Socioemotional wealth and business risks in family-controlled firms: Evidence from Spanish olive oil Mills. *Administrative Science Quarterly, 52*(1), 106–137. https://doi.org/10.2189/asqu.52.1.106

Hamilton, J. T. (1995). Pollution as news: Media and stock market reactions to the toxics release inventory data. *Journal of Environmental Economics and Management, 28*(1), 98–113. https://doi.org/10.1006/jeem.1995.1007

Hart, S. L., & Milstein, M. B. (2003). Creating sustainable value. *Academy of Management Perspectives, 17*(2), 56–67. https://doi.org/10.5465/ame.2003.10025194

Herrera, J., & de las Heras-Rosas, C. (2020). Economic, non-economic and critical factors for the sustainability of family firms. *Journal of Open Innovation: Technology, Market, and Complexity, 6*(4), 1–22. https://doi.org/10.3390/joitmc6040119

Hirigoyen, G., & Poulain-Rehm, T. (2014). The corporate social responsibility of family businesses: An international approach. *International Journal of Financial Studies, 2*(3), 240–265. https://doi.org/10.3390/ijfs2030240

Horváthová, E. (2010). Does environmental performance affect financial performance? A meta-analysis. *Ecological Economics, 70*(1), 52–59. https://doi.org/10.1016/j.ecolecon.2010.04.004

Hussain, N., Rigoni, U., & Cavezzali, E. (2018). Does it pay to be sustainable? Looking inside the black box of the relationship between sustainability performance and financial performance. *Corporate Social Responsibility and Environmental Management, 25*(6), 1198–1211. https://doi.org/10.1002/csr.1631

Jang, S. S., Ko, H., Chung, Y., & Woo, C. (2019). CSR, social ties and firm performance. *Corporate Governance: The International Journal of Business in Society., 19*(6), 1310–1323. https://doi.org/10.1108/CG-02-2019-0068

Jaskiewicz, P., & Klein, S. (2007). The impact of goal alignment on board composition and board size in family businesses. *Journal of Business Research, 60*(10), 1080–1089. https://doi.org/10.1016/j.jbusres.2006.12.015

Kallmuenzer, A., Nikolakis, W., Peters, M., & Zanon, J. (2018). Trade-offs between dimensions of sustainability: Exploratory evidence from family firms in rural tourism regions. *Journal of Sustainable Tourism, 26*(7), 1204–1221. https://doi.org/10.1080/09669582.2017.1374962

Kandel, E., & Lazear, E. P. (1992). Peer pressure and partnerships. *Journal of Political Economy, 100*(4), 801–817. https://doi.org/10.1086/261840

Katmon, N., Mohamad, Z. Z., Norwani, N. M., & Farooque, O. A. (2019). Comprehensive board diversity and quality of corporate social responsibility disclosure: Evidence from an emerging market. *Journal of Business Ethics, 157*(2), 447–481. https://doi.org/10.1007/s10551-017-3672-6

Kellermanns, F. W., & Eddleston, K. A. (2004). Feuding families: When conflict does a family firm good. *Entrepreneurship: Theory and Practice, 28*, 209–228. https://doi.org/10.1111/j.1540-6520.2004.00040.x

Khattak, M. A. (2021). Corporate sustainability and financial performance of banks in Muslim economies: The role of institutions. *Journal of Public Affairs, 21*(1). https://doi.org/10.1002/pa.2156

Kotlar, J., & De Massis, A. (2013). Goal setting in family firms: Goal diversity, social interactions, and collective commitment to family-centered goals. *Entrepreneurship: Theory and Practice, 37*(6), 1263–1288. https://doi.org/10.1111/etap.12065

Kurapatskie, B., & Darnall, N. (2013). Which corporate sustainability activities are associated with greater financial payoffs? *Business Strategy and the Environment, 22*(1), 49–61. https://doi.org/10.1002/bse.1735

Landi, C. G., Rapone, V., Tuccillo, D., & Rey, A. (2019). Does ethics reward on public markets: Empirical evidences ten years after the great recession. *International Journal of Business Administration, 10*(3). https://doi.org/10.5430/ijba.v10n3p1

Landi, G., & Sciarelli, M. (2019). Towards a more ethical market: The impact of ESG rating on corporate financial performance. *Social Responsibility Journal, 15*(1), 11–27. https://doi.org/10.1108/SRJ-11-2017-0254

Le Breton-Miller, I., & Miller, D. (2016). Family firms and practices of sustainability: A contingency view. *Journal of Family Business Strategy, 7*(1), 26–33. https://doi.org/10.1016/j.jfbs.2015.09.001

Lepore, L., Paolone, F., & Cambrea, D. R. (2018). Ownership structure, investors' protection and corporate valuation: The effect of judicial system efficiency in family and non-family firms. *Journal of Management and Governance, 22*, 829–862. https://doi.org/10.1007/s10997-018-9405-0

López-González, E., Martínez-Ferrero, J., & García-Meca, E. (2019). Corporate social responsibility in family firms: A contingency approach. *Journal of Cleaner Production, 211*, 1044–1064. https://doi.org/10.1016/j.jclepro.2018.11.251

López-Pérez, M., Melero-Polo, I., Vázquez-Carrasco, R., & Cambra-Fierro, J. (2018). Sustainability and business outcomes in the context of SMEs: Comparing family firms vs. Non-family firms. *Sustainability, 10*(11), 4080. https://doi.org/10.3390/su10114080

Lu, J., & Herremans, I. M. (2019). Board gender diversity and environmental performance: An industries perspective. *Business Strategy and the Environment, 28*(7), 1449–1464. https://doi.org/10.1002/bse.2326

Lu, L. W., & Taylor, M. E. (2018). A study of the relationships among environmental performance, environmental disclosure, and financial performance. *Asian Review of Accounting, 26*(1), 107–130. https://doi.org/10.1108/ARA-01-2016-0010/FULL/HTML

Lu, W., Chau, K. W., Wang, H., & Pan, W. (2014). A decade's debate on the nexus between corporate social and corporate financial performance: A critical review of empirical studies 2002–2011. *Journal of Cleaner Production, 79*, 195–206. https://doi.org/10.1016/j.jclepro.2014.04.072

Margolis, J. D., & Walsh, J. P. (2003). Misery loves companies: Rethinking social initiatives by business. *Administrative Science Quarterly, 48*(2). https://doi.org/10.2307/3556659

Marques, P., Presas, P., & Simon, A. (2014). The heterogeneity of family firms in CSR engagement: The role of values. *Family Business Review, 27*(3), 206–227. https://doi.org/10.1177/0894486514539004

Martin Curran, M., & Moran, D. (2007). Impact of the FTSE4Good index on firm price: An event study. *Journal of Environmental Management, 82*(4), 529–537. https://doi.org/10.1016/j.jenvman.2006.02.010

Martínez-Ferrero, J., & Frías-Aceituno, J. V. (2015). Relationship between sustainable development and financial performance: International empirical research. *Business Strategy and the Environment, 24*(1), 20–39. https://doi.org/10.1002/bse.1803

Memili, E., Fang, H., Koç, B., Yildirim-Öktem, Ö., & Sonmez, S. (2018). Sustainability practices of family firms: The interplay between family ownership and long-term orientation. *Journal of Sustainable Tourism, 26*(1), 9–28. https://doi.org/10.1080/09669582.2017.1308371

Miller, D., Le Breton-Miller, I., & Lester, R. H. (2009). Family ownership and acquisition behavior in publicly-traded companies. *Strategic Management Journal, 31*(2). https://doi.org/10.1002/smj.802

Miller, D., Le Breton-Miller, I., & Lester, R. H. (2013). Family firm governance, strategic conformity, and performance: Institutional vs. strategic perspectives. *Organization Science, 24*(1), 189–209. https://doi.org/10.1287/orsc.1110.0728

Minichilli, A., Brogi, M., & Calabrò, A. (2016). Weathering the storm: Family ownership, governance, and performance through the financial and economic crisis. *Corporate Governance: An International Review, 24*(6), 552–568. https://doi.org/10.1111/corg.12125

Misani, N., & Pogutz, S. (2015). Unraveling the effects of environmental outcomes and processes on financial performance: A non-linear approach. *Ecological Economics, 109*, 150–160. https://doi.org/10.1016/j.ecolecon.2014.11.010

Nuber, C., Velte, P., & Hörisch, J. (2020). The curvilinear and time-lagging impact of sustainability performance on financial performance: Evidence from Germany. *Corporate Social Responsibility and Environmental Management, 27*(1), 232–243. https://doi.org/10.1002/csr.1795

O'Toole, J., Galbraith, J., & Lawler, E. E. (2002). When two (or more) heads are better than one. The promise and pitfalls of shared leadership. *California Management Review, 44*(4), 65–83. https://doi.org/10.4135/9781452229539.n12

Orazalin, N., & Baydauletov, M. (2020). Corporate social responsibility strategy and corporate environmental and social performance: The moderating role of board gender diversity. *Corporate Social Responsibility and Environmental Management, 27*(4), 1664–1676. https://doi.org/10.1002/csr.1915

Plümper, T., & Troeger, V. E. (2007). Efficient estimation of time-invariant and rarely changing variables in finite sample panel analyses with unit fixed effects. *Political Analysis, 15*(2), 124–139. https://doi.org/10.1093/pan/mpm002

Porter, M. E., & van der Linde, C. (1995). Toward a new conception of the environment–competitiveness relationship. *Journal of Economic Perspectives, 9*, 97–118. https://doi.org/10.1257/jep.9.4.97

Provasi, R., & Harasheh, M. (2021). Gender diversity and corporate performance: Emphasis on sustainability performance. *Corporate Social Responsibility and Environmental Management, 28*(1), 127–137. https://doi.org/10.1002/csr.2037

Rees, W., & Rodionova, T. (2015). The influence of family ownership on corporate social responsibility: An international analysis of publicly listed companies. *Corporate Governance: An International Review., 23*(3), 184–202. https://doi.org/10.1111/corg.12086

Romano, M., Cirillo, A., Favino, C., & Netti, A. (2020). ESG (environmental, social and governance) performance and board gender diversity: The moderating role of CEO duality. *Sustainability, 12*(21), 1–16. https://doi.org/10.3390/su12219298

Rossi, F., & Harjoto, M. A. (2020). Corporate non-financial disclosure, firm value, risk, and agency costs: Evidence from Italian listed companies. *Review of Managerial Science, 14*. https://doi.org/10.1007/s11846-019-00358-z

Rubino, F. E., Tenuta, P., & Cambrea, D. R. (2017). Board characteristics effects on performance in family and non-family business: A multi-theoretical approach. *Journal of Management & Governance, 21*(3), 623–658. https://doi.org/10.1007/s10997-016-9363-3

Ruf, B. M., Muralidhar, K., Brown, R. M., Janney, J. J., & Paul, K. (2001). An empirical investigation of the relationship between change in corporate social performance and financial performance: A stakeholder theory perspective. *Journal of Business Ethics, 32*(2), 143–156. https://doi.org/10.1023/A:1010786912118

Sahut, J. M., Peris-Ortiz, M., & Teulon, F. (2019). Corporate social responsibility and governance. *Journal of Management and Governance, 23*, 901–912. https://doi.org/10.1007/s10997-019-09472-2

Sciarelli, M., Tani, M., Landi, G., & Papaluca, O. (2019). The impact of social responsibility disclosure on corporate financial health: Evidences from some Italian public companies. *International Business Research, 12*(3), 109. https://doi.org/10.5539/ibr.v12n3p109

Seifert, B., Morris, S. A., & Bartkus, B. R. (2003). Comparing big givers and small givers: Financial correlates of corporate philanthropy. *Journal of Business Ethics, 45*(3), 195–211. https://doi.org/10.1023/A:1024199411807

Sekhon, A. K., & Kathuria, L. M. (2019). Analyzing the impact of corporate social responsibility on corporate financial performance: Evidence from top Indian firms. *Corporate Governance: The International Journal of Business in Society., 20*(1), 143–157. https://doi.org/10.1108/CG-04-2019-0135

Singal, M., & Gerde, V. W. (2015). Is diversity management related to financial performance in family firms? *Family Business Review, 28*(3), 243–259. https://doi.org/10.1177/0894486514566012

Surroca, J., Tribó, J. A., & Waddock, S. (2010). Corporate responsibility and financial performance: The role of intangible resources. *Strategic Management Journal, 31*(5), 463–490. https://doi.org/10.1002/smj.820

Trumpp, C., & Guenther, T. (2017). Too little or too much? Exploring U-shaped relationships between corporate environmental performance and corporate financial performance. *Business Strategy and the Environment, 26*(1), 49–68. https://doi.org/10.1002/bse.1900

Veltri, S., Mazzotta, R., & Rubino, F. E. (2021). Board diversity and corporate social performance: Does the family firm status matter? *Corporate Social Responsibility and Environmental Management., 28*(6), 1664–1679. https://doi.org/10.1002/CSR.2136

Venturelli, A., Principale, S., Ligorio, L., & Cosma, S. (2021). Walking the talk in family firms. An empirical investigation of CSR communication and practices. *Corporate Social Responsibility and Environmental Management, 28*(1), 497–510. https://doi.org/10.1002/csr.2064

Wagner, D., Block, J. H., Miller, D., Schwens, C., & Xi, G. (2015). A meta-analysis of the financial performance of family firms: Another attempt. *Journal of Family Business Strategy, 6*(1), 3–13. https://doi.org/10.1016/j.jfbs.2015.01.001

Wagner, M., & Blom, J. (2011). The reciprocal and non-linear relationship of sustainability and financial performance. *Business Ethics: A European Review, 20*(4), 418–432. https://doi.org/10.1111/j.1467-8608.2011.01622.x

Walls, J. L., Berrone, P., & Phan, P. H. (2012). Corporate governance and environmental performance: Is there really a link? *Strategic Management Journal, 33*(8), 885–913. https://doi.org/10.1002/smj

Wang, L., Li, S., & Gao, S. (2014). Do greenhouse gas emissions affect financial performance?–an empirical examination of Australian public firms. *Business Strategy and the Environment, 23*(8), 505–519. https://doi.org/10.1002/bse.1790

Wang, Q., Dou, J., & Jia, S. (2016). A meta-analytic review of corporate social responsibility and corporate financial performance: The moderating effect of contextual factors. *Business and Society, 55*(8), 1083–1121. https://doi.org/10.1177/0007650315584317

Wu, W., Yang, Y., & Zhou, S. (2017). Multinational firms and cash holdings: Evidence from China. *Finance Research Letters, 20*, 184–191. https://doi.org/10.1016/j.frl.2016.09.024

# Chapter 5
# Future Research Directions

**Abstract** This section describes the aspects that have not been developed in detail in the book and which, in turn, represent ideas for future research on the issues of corporate social responsibility and, more specifically, on the importance of implementing social responsibility activities in companies, also considering their ability to affect firm performance.

The book is not without limitations, representing future research opportunities, especially for corporate governance and sustainability scholars.

The descriptive part of the book describes the origins, the historical evolution, and the structure of the rating agencies and the main ESG indexes. However, we did not pay detailed attention to the methodologies used in this area to understand which elements generate divergence in the final results and how this problem can be solved.

While there is complete agreement on the importance of ESG investments, there is a clear divergence on what constitutes a sustainable investment. Since the ESG reporting market is diverse and virtually unregulated, the reliability of ESG assessments is somewhat opaque. Investment choices are guided by ESG ratings, making the construction and disagreement of ESG ratings a central concern. ESG ratings provided by different ESG rating agencies significantly diverge, and associations between the several ESG ratings are generally low. ESG rating providers have become influential institutions. Sustainable investing is rapidly expanding, and mutual funds that invest according to ESG ratings see sizable inflows. This unprecedented demand for assets with superior ESG performance should drive up their prices, but empirical evidence is mixed while theoretical studies suggest this. One of the possible explanations is that the various diverging ESG ratings provided by raters add noise to the market. The disparity in ratings dilutes the impact of ESG performance ratings on asset prices, making it unlikely that ESG performance will be mirrored in share and corporate bond prices. In other words, the ambiguity concerning ESG ratings is an obstacle to the decision-making process that contribute to a sustainable economy.

Furthermore, the ESG rating divergence is caused by a random measurement error and a subjective specific bias of the evaluator. That phenomenon is well known as the halo effect, which states that a firm that receives a high score in one category is

© The Author(s), under exclusive license to Springer Nature Switzerland AG 2022 
P. Tenuta, D. R. Cambrea, *Corporate Sustainability*, SIDREA Series in Accounting and Business Administration, https://doi.org/10.1007/978-3-031-11491-5_5

more likely to receive high scores in all the other categories from the same rater. Several authors argue that these agencies may be motivated to provide inaccurate, inflated, or deflated ratings. The divergence in ESG ratings provided by various rating agencies poses a significant challenge to investors. Relying solely on a single rating provider is a risky procedure. Investors who ignore these issues and base their strategies on the results of a single rating agency may end up investing in a portfolio of companies that are only "subjectively" sustainable.

Despite raising investor and academic awareness of the noisy problems caused by the divergence of various ESG ratings, very few studies attempted to solve the problem. To the best of our knowledge, no studies have provided a single assessment that overcomes current divergences. The interest in corporate sustainability is increasing lately, and sustainability scholars are considering unique aspects that have not been considered before. Therefore, future research can look in detail at each ESG rating, trying to develop a single rating capable of considering all the criteria adopted by the main rating agencies. A more accurate ESG assessment, capable of taking into account the overall ESG assessment of rating agencies, would have highly positive impacts on several branches of subjects (economic, scientific, political, and socio-cultural).

# Chapter 6
# Conclusions

**Abstract** This section of the book reviews all the topics that have been covered in the three chapters in the book. After briefly reviewing the main topics addressed in the book, this paragraph highlights the most relevant conclusions for the scientific community and focuses on the contribution, expressed in terms of greater knowledge of sustainability issues, which the book aims to suggest to all those who show interest in corporate sustainability activities.

Businesses find themselves facing a context in which balance and business success no longer derive exclusively from the pursuit of objectives of an income nature but from compliance with an integrated approach that must necessarily consider the ethical aspect of their management (Allen, 2001; Cassidy, 2003). Leading businesses towards sustainability requires a change in conceiving and measuring one's performance by looking jointly at the three economic, social, and environmental dimensions (Eccles & Krzus, 2010) without emphasizing one aspect over the other (Daddi et al., 2019). From this point of view, the CE becomes essential because it is a key strategy to achieve corporate sustainability (Ghisellini et al., 2016; Murray et al., 2017). Numerous scholars observe that the CE can incentivize companies' sustainable competitive advantage.

According to Aboulamer (2018), the CE produces positive externalities that translate into financial gain for shareholders. Furthermore, investors tend to penalize companies that do not adopt a corporate sustainability strategy (Lourenço et al., 2012).

Companies have understood the need to include environmental, social, and economic sustainability within the different management models (Buxel et al., 2015), which necessarily passes through the implementation of the CE.

In this book, we have analyzed the various determinants that lead companies towards sustainability. At the moment, among the main advocates of corporate sustainability are investors who want to invest in only those companies that have a clear economic expectations and that, at the same time, produce the best ESG performances (Diez-Cañamero et al., 2020). Measuring and reporting corporate performance also looking at environmental, social, and governance aspects has led to the creation of more complex tools to demonstrate one's impact in terms of

© The Author(s), under exclusive license to Springer Nature Switzerland AG 2022 
P. Tenuta, D. R. Cambrea, *Corporate Sustainability*, SIDREA Series in Accounting and Business Administration, https://doi.org/10.1007/978-3-031-11491-5_6

sustainability. Sustainability reporting, ratings, and ESG indexes are among the tools companies use to show their contribution to sustainable development. We analyzed the reporting documents starting from the classic models that separate financial information from non-financial information and then moving on to integrated models (Venturelli et al., 2017), which include both types of information in order to provide stakeholders with overall summary data on the company performance (Maas et al., 2016). We have understood that the trend of recent years is moving towards the final goal of simplifying sustainability reporting and bringing it on a par with financial reporting by strengthening existing regulations. Its proposal for the European Commission's Corporate Sustainability Reporting Directive (CSRD) 2021/0104 extends the scope to all large companies and all companies listed on regulated markets. This would lead to around 50,000 EU companies following the detailed sustainability reporting rules, up from 11,000 today. By identifying separate rules for SMEs, which non-listed SMEs can voluntarily follow.

The analysis of rating agencies and ESG indexes has allowed us to understand their origins, historical evolution, and structure. We have seen a large increase in rating agencies and ESG indexes since the 1990s and several scientific studies contest their measurements. Despite measuring identical performances, ESG ratings and indexes often obtain different results. It is not uncommon to find companies classified in multiple ratings obtaining different and difficult to compare scores (Chatterji et al., 2016; Semenova & Hassel, 2015). This is due to the use by each rating agency of its own methodology and, therefore, the heterogeneity of measurement approaches (Delmas & Blass, 2010; Hedesström et al., 2011) but it is undoubtedly linked to a still excessively high degree of subjectivity. Furthermore, rating agencies and ESG indexes, despite having the objective of developing sustainable business practices, do not do it with disinterest (Escrig-Olmedo et al., 2014). A system that does not validly and reliably reflect the realities of the various companies could have important impacts especially on investors whom unreliable results could mislead. This would nullify the contribution of SRIs to sustainable development (Busch et al., 2016).

We investigated the 40 Milan Exchange companies (FTSE-MIB 40). We find that the relationship between sustainability and financial performance is not statistically significant in our total sample of analyses. Diversely, the relationship becomes negative within the subsample of family firms. The negative and statistically significant relationship in family businesses is positively moderated by the presence of collegiate leadership (plus board members with executive power).

The conclusions reached by the study allow us to state that it is not enough to make investments in sustainability activities in order to have good management results. Therefore, institutional actors should examine all aspects of sustainability policies, taking into account, first of all, the various types and different configurations of businesses present on the market, but above all considering the specific characteristics of the institutional context of reference, before trying to influence the investment decisions of businesses. With regard to family firms, the study suggests that it is difficult for them to translate investments in sustainability into improved performance. However, multiple directors with an executive role is a safeguard for family shareholders, who may benefit from increased firm value.

The contribution of this book is to provide an overview of sustainability concepts and practices and how companies try to apply them because they have become part of their competitive strategy. We fill the gap in the literature by analyzing the origins, historical evolution, and structure of the main rating agencies and the main existing ESG indexes. Furthermore, by analyzing the impact of CS, measured through ESG performance, on corporate financial performance, our research contributes to the existing literature and fills the gaps in the analysis relating to family businesses by adding a relevant element neglected in previous studies, such as the possibility to have more subjects at the top decision-making (co-leadership, a typical feature of Italian family businesses).

## References


Aboulamer, A. (2018). Adopting a circular business model improves market equity value. *Thunderbird International Business Review, 60*(5), 765–769. https://doi.org/10.1002/tie.21922

Allen, W. (2001). The mysterious art of corporate governance. *Corporate Board, 22*, 1–5.

Busch, T., Bauer, R., & Orlitzky, M. (2016). Sustainable development and financial markets: Old paths and new avenues. *Business and Society, 55*(3), 303–329. https://doi.org/10.1177/0007650315570701

Buxel, H., Esenduran, G., & Griffin, S. (2015). Strategic sustainability: Creating business value with life cycle analysis. *Business Horizons, 58*(1), 109–122. https://doi.org/10.1016/j.bushor.2014.09.004

Cassidy, D. (2003). Maximizing shareholder value: The risks to employees, customers and the community. *Corporate Governance: The International Journal of Business in Society, 3*(2), 32–37. https://doi.org/10.1108/14720700310474046

Chatterji, A. K., Durand, R., Levine, D. I., & Touboul, S. (2016). Do ratings of firms converge? Implications for managers, investors and strategy researchers. *Strategic Management Journal, 37*, 1597–1614. https://doi.org/10.1002/smj.2407

Daddi, T., Ceglia, D., Bianchi, G., & de Barcellos, M. D. (2019). Paradoxical tensions and corporate sustainability: A focus on circular economy business cases. *Corporate Social Responsibility and Environmental Management, 26*(4), 770–780. https://doi.org/10.1002/csr.1719

Delmas, M., & Blass, V. D. (2010). Measuring corporate environmental performance: The trade-offs of sustainability ratings. *Business Strategy and the Environment, 19*(4), 245–260. https://doi.org/10.1002/bse.676

Diez-Cañamero, B., Bishara, T., Otegi-Olaso, J. R., Minguez, R., & Fernández, J. M. (2020). Measurement of corporate social responsibility: A review of corporate sustainability indexes, rankings and ratings. *Sustainability, 12*(5). https://doi.org/10.3390/su12052153

Eccles, R. G., & Krzus, M. P. (2010). *One report: Integrated reporting for a sustainable strategy*. Wiley.

Escrig-Olmedo, E., Muñoz-Torres, M. J., Fernández-Izquierdo, M. Á., & Rivera-Lirio, J. M. (2014). Lights and shadows on sustainability rating scoring. *Review of Managerial Science, 8*(4), 559–574. https://doi.org/10.1007/s11846-013-0118-0

Ghisellini, P., Cialani, C., & Ulgiati, S. (2016). A review on circular economy: The expected transition to a balanced interplay of environmental and economic systems. *Journal of Cleaner Production, 114*, 11–32. https://doi.org/10.1016/j.jclepro.2015.09.007

Hedesström, M., Lundqvist, U., & Biel, A. (2011). Investigating consistency of judgement across sustainability analyst organizations. *Sustainable Development, 19*(2), 119–134. https://doi.org/10.1002/sd.511

Lourenço, I. C., Branco, M. C., Curto, J. D., & Eugénio, T. (2012). How does the market value corporate sustainability performance? *Journal of Business Ethics, 108*(4), 417–428. https://doi.org/10.1007/s10551-011-1102-8

Maas, K., Schaltegger, S., & Crutzen, N. (2016). Integrating corporate sustainability assessment, management accounting, control, and reporting. *Journal of Cleaner Production, 136*, 237–248. https://doi.org/10.1016/j.jclepro.2016.05.008

Murray, A., Skene, K., & Haynes, K. (2017). The circular economy: An interdisciplinary exploration of the concept and application in a global context. *Journal of Business Ethics, 140*(3), 369–380. https://doi.org/10.1007/s10551-015-2693-2

Semenova, N., & Hassel, L. G. (2015). On the validity of environmental performance metrics. *Journal of Business Ethics, 132*(2), 249–258. https://doi.org/10.1007/s10551-014-2323-4

Venturelli, A., Caputo, F., Cosma, S., Leopizzi, R., & Pizzi, S. (2017). Directive 2014/95/EU: Are Italian companies already compliant? *Sustainability, 9*(8). https://doi.org/10.3390/su9081385

The manufacturer's authorised representative in the EU is Springer Nature Customer Service Centre GmbH, Europaplatz 3, 69115 Heidelberg, Germany. If you have any concerns regarding our products, please contact ProductSafety@springernature.com

Printed and bound by CPI Group (UK) Ltd, Croydon, CR0 4YY
28/09/2026
02224093-0011